# Early reviews by managers

'They should've had us read this book in business school (instead of teaching us the perfect market theory). This is the most valuable book on management that I have ever read.'
*Darrell Benatar, CEO, UserTesting.com*

'The unique approach of this book results in each chapter hitting the target and teaching a valuable lesson. There's more truly useful content in this concise resource than much lengthier management books that I've read.'
*Steve Brazier, Director of Education, Promethean Ltd.*

'More content, more wisdom and less words to read. When our managers read this book, life at work becomes more productive and a lot less hassle for everyone.'
*Mike Faith, President & CEO, Headsets.com, Inc.*

'Stuart Wyatt provides direct, straightforward, no-holds-barred observations. Stuart Wyatt tells it like it is.'
*Daniel Robins, Commuter Services Manager,*
*Parsons Brinkerhoff*

'As I floundered on my tenth day as a new manager (in 2003), I read an early draft of this book and it helped me re-frame my thinking around management and leadership. By the end of the month, and after several reads through, I considered myself a manager. I came back to the book so many times that I started using it as a training tool for managers on my team. Now, this book is required reading for any supervisor or manager on my team. I keep four business books next to my desk for quick reference – *The Secret Laws of Management* is one of them.

Wyatt has found a way to cram leadership and manage-ment wisdom into brief, concise and digestible descriptions. Without a doubt, these have been the best 142 pages for my leadership career.'
*Chris Hicken, General Manager, Headsets.com, Inc.*

'I am very impressed with this book. It has muscle and sinew that have been exercised in real-life competition. Tightly written, no holds barred. Every executive could use it as a tune-up checklist. When the book is published, I will buy it for my staff. A standout piece of work.'

*Anthony Sandberg, President, OCSC Sailing*

'This book is ideal for CEOs and their management teams to use as a workbook, a powerful tool for sharpening up performance and improving management skills.'

*Michael A. Torres, CEO, Adelante Capital Management LLC.*

'Fits the bill as an insightful and motivating primer for managers looking to win.'

*Stephen Jury, Vice Chairman of Education Strategy, Promethean Ltd.*

'This is the way all business books should be written, with compelling ideas organized in a real-world way. As you face the daily challenges of managing or leading you can return to this book for inspiration and practical ideas for almost any challenge. I am only sorry that I am reading a pre-release copy, as I cannot wait to share the ideas in this book with my entire management team.

We acquired a company this year and this book should be required reading for anyone who is planning an acquisition or merger. The section on change is particularly relevant to the bringing together of two companies.'

*Justin Hersh, CEO, Group Delphi*

'The individual laws are too true. I really like the honesty. A great tool for training . . . so easy to read and use as a management tool and reference. Every manager should have one on their desk.'

*Franka Winchester, General Partner, Pacific Crest Group*

'Stuart Wyatt has written a first-class management support tool, based on his many years of experience. I particularly like the From problem to solution section, which makes it easy for busy managers to get to the law they need that will help them with their specific management problems.'

*Barry Faith, CEO, Arlington Associates*

# The Secret Laws
# of Management

*40 Essential Truths for Managers*

*by*
*Stuart Wyatt*

**headline**
business plus

First published in 2010 by
HEADLINE PUBLISHING GROUP

1

Cataloguing in Publication Data is available from
the British Library

ISBN 978 0 7553 6094 9

Typeset in Palatino by Avon DataSet Ltd,
Bidford-on-Avon, Warwickshire

Printed in the UK by CPI Mackays, Chatham, ME5 8TD

Headline's policy is to use papers that are natural, renewable and
recyclable products and made from wood grown in sustainable
forests. The logging and manufacturing processes are expected to
conform to the environmental regulations of the country of origin.

HEADLINE PUBLISHING GROUP
An Hachette UK Company
338 Euston Road
London NW1 3BH

www.headline.co.uk
www.hachette.co.uk

# Contents

## The Laws

'There is an English proverb that says there are no bad students, only bad teachers. I believe it also applies to a company. There are no bad employees, only bad managers.'

*Dr T. S. Lin, 1918–2006,*
*CEO of Tatung Company for 30 years*

# Acknowledgements

I wish to thank Mike Faith, my agent Robin Wade, John Moseley at Headline and my wife and proof-reader, Terri. Without them, this book would not exist.

I also wish to thank the many managers who have given helpful feedback as the book developed, including Barry Faith, Chris Hicken, Courtney Wight, Daniel Robins, Joseph Pianetta, Ken Nash, Shaun Masterman, Shawn Gwinnett, Stephen Jury, Steve Brazier and Wayne Downer.

*Secret:*

> A central but sometimes elusive principle ...
> An underlying explanation that is unknown or
> unobserved by others ... A method of formula
> on which success is based.

*Law:*

> A rule or manner of behaviour that is
> instinctive or spontaneous ... A general prin-
> ciple, formula or rule describing a pheno-
> menon.

*From the American Heritage*
*and Collins dictionaries*

# Four ways to profit from this book

1. **Read as usual**
2. **Dip in and read in any order**
   Each law is a short read with its own
   stand-alone message.
3. **Be your own coach and mentor**
   Read each law, one at a time. Review your
   management practice. How does this law apply
   to you and your team? Can the suggestions help
   you to manage your team more effectively and
   improve performance?
4. **Solve management problems**
   Use the list of common management problems at
   the rear of this book to point you towards the
   relevant laws that will help diagnose likely
   causes and find practical solutions.

# Introduction

Dear Reader,

Every team comprises a group of people with unique personalities. However, as people work together, a similar set of problems keeps on reappearing. The people are diverse, the jobs vary considerably, the culture of each organization is unique, but many of the people-related challenges remain the same.

This book identifies 40 laws of management, essential truths about managing people. Each law presents a common or inescapable challenge that managers must face. Failing to recognize and handle the challenge would lead to one or more problems, including reduced productivity, discord among team members and the manager's life at work becoming most disagreeable.

Being aware of these laws enables us to avoid many of the pitfalls that other managers fall into headlong. The outcome is less personal strain, improved results and effective relationships between team members. By effective relationships, I don't refer to close friendship and a cosy good time for all, but to mutual respect among team members. Respect is built upon the manager maintaining a reasonable degree of harmony while leading the team to achieve things together. And achieving things together provides the glue that quickly bonds effective relationships within a team.

When the team enjoys effective relationships,

they arrive for work each morning full of positive anticipation, rather than merely working the necessary hours, earning their pay and looking forward to going home.

As you read the laws, I expect that you will often find yourself thinking, 'Yes, I've seen that for myself.' At other times, you may need convincing. However, I offer only short explanations. I imagine you to be a very busy person who just wants the facts, plain and simple, quick and easy to read or consult when you face a new challenge. So, when you feel the need for extra proof to corroborate the content of this book, I suggest you give greatest credence to the evidence of your own eyes. Observe the people who surround you at work. You have daily access to indisputable evidence that these laws of management are a practical reality, verifiable through experience and observation.

I present each law, explain it briefly and suggest ideas on the smart ways for a manager to act. I don't claim that my suggestions on what to do about each law will be universally appropriate. You must use your own judgement in each situation. However, I do assert that if you ignore the laws of management, you will find your job much harder than it need be, and you won't achieve all that you could.

The laws apply to many aspects of management and leadership. The actions I suggest in response to one law may also be sensible management practice in other situations. Therefore, you'll find that the core concepts appear several times in different ways. I make no apologies for this repetition, because many people find that helpful.

I hope you enjoy reading *The Secret Laws of Management*. May I be a little bit cheeky and remind you of the obvious? It's not the reading that improves performance, but the action that follows.

*Stuart Wyatt*

'*I hear and I forget.*
*I see and I remember.*
*I do and I understand.*'

*Confucius, 551 BC–479 BC,*
*Chinese philosopher, founder of Confucianism*

# Law 1

# People tolerate being managed, but they love being led

It's the foremost law; people tolerate being managed, but love being led. First, consider how often you have heard people complaining to each other about management.

One might expect staff to rebel against poor management, but they rarely do so. One strident employee may say, *'We'll tell them.'* But if he opens his mouth to complain, and then looks over his shoulder for support, suddenly he finds himself standing alone.

People often complain to each other about their manager but open mutiny is almost unheard of. This is probably the main reason why so many incompetent managers continue to have free rein to make people's life at work so disagreeable. Working for an inept manager can be very unpleasant. It can also be very frustrating because his or her incompetence holds back your own performance. You may even appear to be responsible for his or her mistakes, making you look foolish in front of clients, suppliers or co-workers.

Working for a manager of only average ability is not much better, yet people tolerate this and get on with their job. When the manager is fully competent, then people respond by doing a competent job. Good management elicits competent performance because people know what to do, by when and to what standard of performance. And their personal effort is coordinated with the work of those around them. But is that good enough?

Consider how the following descriptors highlight the essential difference between management and leadership at work:

*Manage:*

> *run, direct, administer, supervise, deal with, handle, control.*

*Lead:*

> *guide, show the way, direct, pilot, escort, go in front, go ahead, conduct.*

Management without leadership produces only a competent performance because, although the manager organizes the team efficiently, the team is not motivated to give their very best.

Add leadership and now people feel inspired to try harder. Performance lifts to much higher levels. When people work for a good leader they feel encouraged, supported and believed in. They want to contribute all that they are capable of, and they feel positive about the future. They feel less controlled, more encouraged. This empowering experience increases team enthusiasm and energy levels and helps create an expectation that the team will do well.

But leadership alone is not enough. Leadership without management will fail through a lack of coordinated direction. Management and leadership together spark off the highest levels of achievement. Both leader and team enjoy the buzz they feel from achieving things together, which is why people love to work for a first-rate leader.

The best leaders do more than merely organize and control their people. Either through instinct, or by intelligent thought, they know how to handle each situation so that the ordinary people around them produce extraordinary results.

If you have been fortunate enough to work for one of these leaders, you will remember how you felt motivated to go the extra mile and give your best. You will have found working with them more enjoyable, not necessarily fun-filled days, but fulfilling because you achieved so much, which was extremely satisfying. When working for this person you felt motivated and confident of your success.

Effective leaders do not work extra hard. In fact, they often appear more relaxed and easy-going, but they are very active people setting the agenda through being intelligently proactive, and intelligently reacting to events and people issues as they occur.

The quickest way to learn leadership is on the job and the following 39 essential truths provide a resource to help you decide when to be proactive or reactive, on which issues and how to go about it.

*'Divide and rule, a sound motto.*
*Unite and lead, a better one.'*

> *Johann Wolfgang von Goethe, 1749–1832,*
> *possibly Germany's greatest writer, especially*
> *in philosophy, humanism and science*

# Law 2
## Deadlines often backfire

Jim, a member of the team, asks, *'When do you need this done by?'* The team leader quickly replies, *'By end Friday.'* It seems so simple. The pressure of the deadline will spur on Jim to be more productive. Actually, it may have the opposite effect.

The very word *deadline* is overdramatic because in business nobody dies when the line is crossed. We all miss deadlines; life goes on, so why worry? Humour the boss, agree to the deadline if you must, avoid it if you can, do your best, or don't even try, it makes little difference. That attitude is all too frequent. Many bosses will bury their heads in the sand and deny it, but it is a common scenario.

Frequently, managers set deadlines simply to put pressure on their people to get the job done more quickly. But be warned, deadlines frequently backfire. Imagine yourself in this situation.

You lead a department within a large organization. The CEO sets you an objective. He wants this achieved by end next week. It seems practical and so you agree. Or, at least, you don't say that you may not be able to achieve his deadline. You're not worried; it's not too much work for your team.

However, as you get into the detail of the job you find that in order to complete the task you need another department to supply essential information. Snag!

You approach the manager of the other department but she says, '*Sorry, I'd like to help, but getting that information would take time, and right now all my people are too busy working on other stuff. I have this important job to do for the CEO and I must get that done on time!*' In the end, she completes her task for the CEO, right on time, and you don't. The moral of the story is that you can only be confident of meeting a deadline if you control all the people and resources necessary to do the job. The same is true for your own staff.

So, returning to Jim, and that deadline set for him to complete by end Friday: was Jim able to do the entire job himself, or might he be relying upon help from somebody else? If so, then Jim may have an impossible deadline. That's a real backfire, because impossible deadlines lead to inevitable disappointment, dissatisfaction and feelings of failure. Jim will resent this, quietly, and next time he is set a deadline Jim will be on his guard. He will try to avoid commitment, perhaps issuing a soft warning of failure by saying, '*I'll try.*' If his manager takes Jim through the loop several times, repeatedly setting impossible deadlines, so that Jim repeatedly fails and feels the pain, then Jim is going to try every trick that he can think of in order to avoid any work that involves deadlines, just to avoid the certain pain of failure. Or Jim may become expert at shifting the blame elsewhere; creating a team that is more concerned with shunning responsibility than getting work done.

The second type of deadline that backfires

frequently concerns creative work. It would be unrealistic to have expected Einstein to discover new laws of physics to a fixed timescale. He discovered the Law of Relativity through creative thought, not a measurable amount of work. Creative inspirations and accidental discoveries don't pop into the mind on a predetermined timescale. If you were asked to design a new advertisement within seven days, it should be possible. The degree of creativity need not be high because you can adapt and borrow ideas from past successful advertisements. However, if we modify the objective slightly and ask you to create a truly original concept, that may or may not happen easily. Often, after several days' hard graft on the project, a brilliant new idea pops into your head while you are relaxing at home, but you can't be sure this will happen. Truly original thoughts will not present themselves to a timetable.

Douglas Adams, the author, joked about his publisher's deadlines like this: *'I love deadlines; I love the whooshing sound they make as they pass by!'* Don't let your deadlines become a joke.

There are helpful deadlines and counter-productive deadlines. When you are about to set a deadline, always stop, pause, and think before you act:

- Do set deadlines when the person responsible for achieving the objective has direct control over all the people and resources necessary to complete the job, and you can make a reasonably accurate assessment of how long the job should take

- Don't set deadlines when you need to achieve objectives that rely upon the cooperation of people outside your control. Instead, set targets and objectives, but not with deadlines
- Do encourage higher productivity by making the targets and deadlines stretching, but achievable
- Don't let your desire for productivity lead you to lose touch with reality
- Don't set artificial deadlines for truly original creative work, but do engender enthusiasm and urgency
- When you need to achieve a major objective that requires the cooperation of people outside your control, break down the major objective into mini-objectives. Consider setting realistic but stretching deadlines for each of the mini-objectives that fall within your area of control
- When mini-objectives rely upon input from customers, suppliers, other departments, etc., try to be realistic and do all that you can to minimize delays caused by others
- If you want your team to feel motivated by the deadlines that you set, then you must personally demonstrate that you don't just pluck them out of thin air

Be optimistic but realistic. Never set, or accept, a deadline in haste. Think and plan.

'I have always found that plans are useless, but planning is indispensable.'

Dwight David Eisenhower, 1890–1969,
34th President of the United States of America

# Law 3
## People don't say NO
## to interruptions often enough

Looking back, the day feels like one long series of interruptions and much of the work planned for the day remains uncompleted. Does that apply to you, or to any of your team?

Of course, many of the interruptions will have been short and well-justified exchanges between you and colleagues, suppliers or customers. And when you are a manager, people refer to you more often.

Some interruptions are urgent and important situations that you need to deal with immediately. Some will be people relying on easy access to your knowledge, too lazy to invest time in learning. Many interruptions will be downright time-wasters. Occasionally, team members will interrupt you to seek your approval before they act, rather than have the confidence to make their own decision, or take personal responsibility.

Many of us accept interruptions without first pausing to think. We often feel the rapidity of the day's events prevents us from pausing long enough to take time to consider how we should react. It seems quicker to accept the interruption and quickly deal with it, and then we find ourselves dragged into countless minor issues, all eating up our day until we have achieved very little.

We have only three potential responses to any interruption, namely the three acts:

*Act now*
*Act later*
*Act never*

Immediately you receive an interruption, pause for a split second and ask yourself, '*Should I act now, act later or act never?*' Having decided the best of these three options, you either:

1. Accept the interruption (act now)
2. Schedule the task for later (act later)
3. Or simply say NO (act never)

Naturally, when we say NO we do it in a considerate way, because although we may need to be ruthless about our use of time we should still aim to be polite in our dealings with others.

The habit of always asking yourself should I act now, act later or act never stops your train of thought for just long enough for wisdom to prevail. The brain has the ability to act wisely, but only if consulted.

If you decide to act now, you first put aside the papers on your desk or turn away from your computer, mentally switching from your train of thought. You deal with the emergency and then re-focus yourself to pick up from where you left off.

If you decide to act later, you diarize future action or set a reminder, or add another item to your to-do list. It is important to recognize how often you need to choose the final option of act never.

Many interruptions bring with them extra work for you. Consider this: would you prefer a busy colleague to admit, *'I want to help, but I don't have the capacity right now,'* or for them to say, *'OK, I'll do it,'* only to let you down later when they find that they do not have the capacity to deliver on their promise?

And frequently, when you say to a team member, *'Not now, I'll speak with you later,'* and then later in the day you ask them what they wanted, they reply, *'Oh, don't worry, I couldn't wait, so I coped by myself.'*

Saying NO wisely can teach your team members to be more independent and more productive. It can be the most effective response. Do you say NO often enough?

*'Respond intelligently, even to unintelligent treatment.'*

*Lao-Tzu, 4th century BC, philosopher of ancient China, central figure in Taoism*

# Law 4
## People don't hit invisible targets, unless by accident

People do not hit targets or achieve business objectives that they don't know about or cannot see. This is self-evident. It's so obvious that one wonders why managers so often overlook this basic fact. For example, here's a common situation.

Imagine you are the member of a team and your manager has convened a team meeting. The manager announces new objectives, perhaps with a slick presentation including pictures or graphs or bar charts, followed by handouts or emailed confirmations. At the time, this all feels very important and probably engenders a positive and animated response. The manager addresses questions and the team returns to getting on with their day-to-day jobs. Some team members file the handouts; some place them on top of mounting stacks of paper; some put them into filing trays. Your team may read your follow-up emails, but usually they give them only a quick scan. They then drag them into folders containing hundreds of other emails, all filed away for potential future reference and quickly forgotten.

After a busy week or two, the meeting soon fades into the back of the memory. The big launch meeting was a one-off event, punctuating a steady flow of familiar work. It's easy for the importance to slide. The manager has probably devoted hours to the objective: discussions with the boss and other managers, and then preparing the team meeting. But for the team, life goes on as usual.

To ensure that every team member shares an equally clear vision, the manager needs to take action that is much more definite. You need them to know who must achieve what, by when, to what standard and possibly at what cost. Hearing the objective once and receiving it in writing is just not enough to penetrate through the mass of other business to become a priority.

Consider you and your own team's current objectives. Do you personally know exactly what you are trying to achieve? Have you defined the targets clearly? In your own mind, do you know what achieving the objective will look like and feel like? Can you immediately list your current objectives without referring to notes? If you can reply to these questions with quick and accurate answers, you're on your way to success. Now think about your team. Does each team member share your clarity of vision? If you asked any one of them to list the current objectives, in descending order of importance, could they do so? And would their list be the same as yours?

If your team passes this test with flying colours, I must congratulate you. You are one in a thousand and on the road to success.

If not, you need to accept that your team is almost certainly going to fail to hit the targets, unless by sheer fluke, extreme good luck or accident.

It is a profound truth that the main reason individuals achieve their goals is because they set them in the first place and then frequently review them in detail, visualizing themselves achieving their objective. Having that vision guides and directs your actions, making it so much easier to achieve the goal and hit the target.

Ensure that each team member knows what they must achieve, split down from major goal into minor tasks, all adding up to achieving each major objective. Next, make your objectives clearly visible to your team by defining the important targets in writing. Keep it short. One side of one page should be the maximum for any one target. That discipline keeps the wording concise, to the point and memorable. People start to forget anything longer than one page. Describe the target, the timescale, the standard of performance required, the means for measuring success and any other supporting detail that is necessary. And then you must do more.

Talk about the target frequently, ensuring that it doesn't become yesterday's news. Build a memorable picture of success. Every team member needs to understand how he or she fits into the overall picture. Each person should know exactly how their personal contribution combines with their teammates' in order to ensure overall team success.

Refer to the written targets regularly and review individual progress with each person. This will prevent the vision from fading, so the end goal remains in sight.

The discipline of fixing goals in writing and revisiting them helps to compel you personally to think through the detail of how to coordinate your team. It also helps you adapt to new circumstances and inevitable challenges as they arise, potentially slowing down progress or pushing you off course.

Naturally, this all makes work for the manager to do, but the time invested will be rewarded manifold.

*'If you don't know where you're going, you'll probably end up somewhere else.'*

*Laurence J. Peter, 1919–1990,*
*American educator and author of* The Peter Principle

# Law 5

# People do not cope with more than seven concurrent objectives

If you have only one job to complete you will have no choice but to give that job your undivided attention. When you concentrate all your effort upon one thing at a time, it is easier to be more effective. If you must divide your time between two objectives, you must keep two balls in the air at the same time without dropping one as you switch your attention between the two jobs.

Every time you switch between jobs, you lose a little momentum. You need to mentally and physically put aside the paraphernalia of the one task and pick up from where you left off on the other. Each job switch drains a little of your momentum, so that your productivity suffers.

Add a third job to your list of concurrent tasks and you need to concentrate a little more on the job-switching process and a little less on the jobs themselves. As you add more jobs, there comes a critical point when the number of jobs you have on the go requires you to become as focused on job-switching as on the tasks themselves. At this point productivity takes a sudden dive. Research has shown that people reach the critical point at seven concurrent tasks for women and five for men. Sorry if that appears sexist, but the research found that most women are more adept than men are at coping with a variety of concurrent tasks.

Coincidentally, how often do you see a juggler manage to keep more than five objects in the air for any length of time? The limit is reputed to be mental, rather than one of physical agility. Many jugglers can handle five balls. Of those, fewer than 40 per cent can manage six, fewer than 30 per cent seven balls, and the few who can juggle seven or more generally keep all the balls in the air for only seconds, not minutes. At work, we often hear how people struggle to *'keep all their balls in the air'* or how they *'dropped the ball'*.

Many world-class top executives successfully manage more than seven concurrent tasks, but these are truly exceptional people and when you examine how they do it, you inevitably find that they employ people solely to help them organize their time and maintain high personal productivity.

You obtain higher productivity from people when you have them focus upon a small number of tasks or objectives. Too few, and some people find their work repetitive and boring, so their enthusiasm is reduced and their productivity falls. Too many, and people start *dropping the ball*.

When you set objectives and tasks for members of your team, avoid job descriptions that contain long lists of catch-all responsibilities. Instead, give each team member clear written objectives, with an absolute maximum of seven, and a realistic maximum of five. Even better, restrict the list to three! That way you make it very much more likely that you'll get the results that you want.

'The test of a first-rate intelligence is the ability to hold two opposed ideas in the mind at the same time, and still retain the ability to function.'

F. Scott Fitzgerald, 1896–1940, American writer

# Law 6
# 1 employee + 2 managers
# = half the output

When you report to two managers, all three of you achieve much less. With two managers, your output will almost certainly halve. And eventually the three of you will probably have a spat. When this happens, productivity will take a further dive.

Think back to your childhood. When you have two managers, it is like having a mother and father. Mum says, *'No ice cream today'*, so you ask Dad for ice cream. He says, *'Great idea, let's all have ice cream.'* Now mother and father have an argument over how to bring up children.

Next, Mum decides that it's time to encourage you to develop a work ethic so she says, *'Today, I'd like you to help me around the house.'* Dad comes along and says, *'What are you doing? I told you yesterday that today you must clean your bicycle!'*

Mother and father have no alternative but to get together and solve the problem that their child has two bosses. If they are good and loving parents they will succeed in coping, but the problem never entirely goes away. And most children learn the valuable lesson of accepting some of the little injustices in life. If you think that adults at work don't act like kids and parents, take a cool analytical look at what goes on around you. They surely do!

Organization structures that create dual reporting

responsibilities work fine if the reporting involves only the giving of information, but when it also involves receiving instructions from two or more sources, it encourages conflict. One manager will be disappointed when his or her work is not completed. Setting realistic deadlines becomes impossible, because no one manager has a full understanding of the person's workload. One boss will tend to pressure for his or her work to be done first.

If you are involved in this problem, do not try to live with it, because you cannot ultimately succeed in this situation. Instead, find a way to eliminate it. The problem of having two managers must not be there in the first place. Eliminate the problem and you will see relationships improve and productivity rise.

*'A boat can't have two captains.'*

*Akira Mori, b.1936,*
*President and CEO of Mori Trust Co.*

# Law 7
## Good managers are occasionally unpopular

Most, if not all of us, care about what others think of us. It is natural that we should wish for others to like us, including those who work for us. For that reason, many managers feel an inner need to be popular with their team.

Almost all people share a common need for approval. It started as young children, when we felt the need for parental approval. And then, during school life, we wanted our classmates to accept and like us. By the time that we reach adulthood, we have a deeply embedded need for others to like us.

This inherent need for approval leads many managers to try too hard to be popular and that eventually creates problems. You do not have to be remote and cold, but you must find the right balance between friendly and cool; you need a balance that fits with your own personality and with your particular management role.

The first potential pitfall is concerning trust. For example, consider this situation, which you may have already experienced. Your boss asks if you had a great weekend. You reply and exchange a few brief words before moving on to talking about work.

Being polite is definitely preferable to being rude or uncivil, so you welcome your boss's approach. However, there is a difference between genuine interest and mere polite conversation.

You have no difficulty discerning if your boss is genuinely interested in you or merely being polite. We make these judgements without conscious effort, and our brain communicates its decision to us instantly, experienced as gut feelings.

Almost all adults are smart enough to see through managers who attempt to ingratiate themselves. At first, the team appreciates that the manager is making an effort to win their approval. But soon, when the manager is displaying symptoms of insincerity, the team starts to become suspicious. Suspicion is very close to mistrust, and nobody gives their best for someone they do not trust.

The second pitfall concerns manipulation. When things go wrong, and the manager's behaviour suddenly switches from being over-friendly to over-cold, the sharp contrast leads some people to view the manager as insincere, two-faced, uncaring and manipulative. This reaction is not necessarily justified, but that's how many people react. You don't want your team to class you as manipulative.

The third pitfall concerns making enemies out of friends. When one team member is a genuine close friend of the manager, eventually, the inevitable happens. Every manager has to occasionally impose an unpopular measure, or deliver a harsh review of performance. Or even worse, the manager must handle a situation when a team member has done something seriously wrong. The manager must discipline that person; even warn them that their actions could lead to dismissal. If the disciplining manager and the employee at fault are close friends, this adds an unpredictable dimension to the problem. The employee often feels unjust and undue resentment that cannot be resolved. Close friends torn apart by conflict often become enemies, and you definitely don't want to create an enemy within your team.

The fourth pitfall concerns apparent favouritism. The team will assume, rightly or wrongly, that a member of the team who enjoys a close personal relationship with their manager is receiving favours and privileges denied to other team members. This encourages other team members to want to be equally well liked. They start devoting more time to ingratiating themselves with their boss than to doing their job. Others react by becoming surly, remote and uncooperative. Both reactions kill productivity and make life at work unpleasant.

The solution to these pitfalls is to be polite, professional and even-handed. Never feign friendliness or interest. Gain respect by consistently doing your best to be a good leader. Over the long haul, people will respect you for this and follow your lead.

Every manager is called upon to be unpopular for some of the time. It goes with the job. However, although you cannot always be popular, you can always be respected, which matters much, much more.

'To avoid criticism, do nothing, say nothing,
and be nothing.'

Elbert Hubbard, 1856–1915,
American writer and philosopher

# Law 8

# People are outrageously optimistic when they estimate time

If we repeat the same task many times we eventually become highly skilled at judging how long a similar task will take to complete. We are no longer estimating based upon little or no knowledge but forecasting based upon knowledge and expertise. Experience has taught us many of the less obvious difficulties that we may encounter, and our detailed knowledge enables us to forecast accurately the time required for each component of the job, and then to combine this information to calculate the total time required. This is how the experienced construction company that quotes a fixed price to erect a skyscraper is capable of planning the hours of labour required to an accuracy of within one per cent. But for unfamiliar tasks, it is very different.

When you ask your people to estimate the time it will take them to complete an unfamiliar task, you should expect them to be outrageously optimistic. Their guesstimate is likely to be wildly inaccurate. An unfair generalization? No.

You can easily check on this for yourself. First, check your own estimating ability. Look through your list of jobs to do. Select one that you are familiar with, and note the time it should take to complete the job. Next, re-scan your list of jobs and find the least familiar task. How long will it take you? Note down your estimates and check your accuracy when both jobs are complete.

Similarly, have team members give you an estimate of the time required for them to complete all of the tasks on their to-do list. You are certain to discover that you work with very optimistic people! This is probably a good trait, because optimists achieve more in life than pessimists do. However, as manager, you need to work with realistic estimates of how long tasks will take. Otherwise, you will have your team attempt the impossible and be doomed to fail. You need to know when to adjust the time estimates that you receive and by how much. Here are some useful guidelines that prove surprisingly accurate:

- If one of your team undertakes a job for the first time, and they can focus upon the work full time, double their most pessimistic time estimate
- If, in parallel, they must also continue with other work, triple their pessimistic estimate. Yes, triple it!
- If a job also relies to any significant degree upon the input of people who do not report to you personally, ask each of them how long they will need to deliver their contribution, and then allow at least double the time they estimate

Try it. You may be surprised how realistic these rules of thumb prove to be. And, in the process, you will avoid suffering the many consequential problems caused by completing jobs later than expected. And when you tell your own boss how long it will realistically take to achieve an objective, you have a fighting chance of becoming the popular one who delivers on time.

*'Let our advance worrying become advance thinking and planning.'*

*Winston Churchill, 1874–1965,*
*British Prime Minister during the Second World War*

# Law 9
## Inertia sets in after
## only fifteen minutes

It takes only about a quarter of an hour for the current prevailing mood of your team to become the short-term norm. For example . . .

Observe that when the team arrives each day to commence work, the first fifteen minutes make a big impact upon the mood for the entire morning, perhaps even the whole day.

In many offices the team starts the day with a leisurely coffee while swapping pleasant social banter: *'Did you see so-and-so on television last night?'* A short discussion about sport, television, movies, the commute, etc. seems only polite. And why not start the day in a relaxed frame of mind?

Unfortunately, this relaxed atmosphere fosters a low productivity situation that lingers on. Once the mood is set, it requires a blast of incoming phone calls, or an immediate crisis, or someone displaying effervescent enthusiasm to break the inertia and set a new tempo.

On the other hand, if the team uses the first few minutes of the day to move quickly from polite chat to productive action, then this day inevitably proves to be a great day for getting things done.

Inertia dictates that when people start moving they keep on moving at the same rate, until some event or happening shakes them out of their current mood. The critical times for a relaxed pace to set in are: first thing in the morning as people arrive for work, coffee time, after lunch time and towards the end of the day. All that adds up to a large proportion of the working day.

The tempo for a creative studio may need to be relaxed and contemplative. Some artists produce their best work when listening to music. But such a laid-back atmosphere will probably not be suited to your office. For example, a team brainstorming session may produce ideas that are more useful when the tempo is mad, rapid and wacky!

The atmosphere and tempo need to match the objectives and the type of team that you're managing. What's the best tempo for your team? The manager has the responsibility for starting the day rolling along at an appropriate pace for the job at hand, then maintaining a productive pace throughout the day.

> *'An object at rest tends to stay at rest and an object in motion tends to stay in motion with the same speed and in the same direction unless acted upon by an unbalanced force.'*
>
> *Newton's First Law of Motion,*
> *Isaac Newton, 1643–1727*

# Law 10
## People hate change
## and change happens

The prosperity of the entire nation is either increasing or decreasing. Study any graph that measures performance and repeatedly you find that the wealth of nations, the profitability of companies, the stock market, the measurable achievements of sportsmen and women are either declining or improving. Reassuringly, graphs generally chart an improvement over time.

Change is inevitable and we all accept that the world moves on. Yet, at work, most people prefer life to remain constant, unchanging and comfortable. But life doesn't work like that.

A plethora of changing conditions impacts upon every organization. All managers learn they must accept constant change as necessary and inevitable. The smart managers see every change as an opportunity and they search for ways to exploit changes to their advantage. This attitude is essential to being a successful manager. You may welcome change as a revitalizing opportunity. You may see new initiatives as a great way to rekindle your personal enthusiasm, but you would be wise to take into account that some of your team probably see things very differently.

In general, employees remain employees when they do not cope too well with the changes that affect their working practices. You need to show respect for people's aversion to change, but still make changes whenever necessary. People's reluctance to accept change remains a difficult problem for leaders in all fields, and the following eight strategies should help you cope with the challenge:

- Condition your team to tolerate a certain amount of change each year as something unavoidable. Remind them in advance that frequent change is an unalterable fact of life and that you expect them to cope with inevitable changes and look for positive advantages. That way, you can raise acceptance levels in advance

- Avoid unnecessary changes. *If it ain't broke, don't fix it* may be a cliché but it remains true. Many companies initiate regular change when it's not necessary. Make sure the changes are steps forward, not merely upsetting employees by unnecessarily stepping sideways or backwards

- Make sure that you correct people when you hear them say how they expect no more changes for a while. Good humouredly remind them of the realities of life

- When you implement a change, do show that you respect others' dislike for change as an understandable point of view. Acknowledging other people's right to hold different opinions often defuses their objections

- Explain why the change must happen. This will

help people to adjust their thinking from aversion to acceptance

- Never begin to make changes, then assume because you have played your part that everything will follow through to a satisfactory conclusion. That would be an abdication of responsibility. Your team will feel you have dumped new problems upon them and just walked away. Instead, be sure to manage the change right through to a fully satisfactory conclusion
- As you implement changes, be on the lookout for things that do not go as planned. Team members may be keen to leap upon minor hiccups as examples that prove the changes were undesirable. React by calmly sorting the problem and restating the eventual advantages
- Finally, look for opportunities to reward people for their contribution to making a success of the change; never forget to give praise where praise is due

*'It is not necessary to change. Survival is not mandatory!'*

*Professor W. Edwards Deming, 1900–1993, American statistician, widely respected in Japan for teaching top management to improve design, product quality and sales*

# Law 11
## People value praise above money

There is a threshold of earnings below which this law does not hold true. However, as soon as earnings exceed that threshold this law is universally true. Consider this.

First, we need to earn enough money to support our basic needs. We each set an individual minimum standard for what we personally consider an acceptable standard of living. Thus, we fix our minimum earnings level. If our income is below this minimum level, raising our income becomes a top priority.

A few people set their personal minimum survival level outrageously high, a champagne lifestyle. They are hooked on the drug of high living. That sort of person must achieve a high salary plus all the possible commissions, bonuses and benefits in order to support their lifestyle. Offer them bonuses for meeting targets and they will work their socks off for you. By the way, this type of person may also devote considerable thought to finding ways to cheat the system. They look for a chink in the fine detail of the bonus scheme that could enable them technically to meet your definition of success and claim their bonus, while actually delivering minimum results. Therefore, when you write bonus plans or commission schemes keep it simple. Be extra careful about how you define the scheme and the rewards, bonus or commissions.

Once we've achieved the lifestyle we consider our comfortable minimum, although extra money is welcome, success and praise motivates us much more. We take pleasure in receiving genuine and heartfelt praise, and we are ready to work extremely hard to receive that praise.

Similarly, if you ask a rich man why he continues to work he never replies, '*I want more money.*' He always talks about fulfilment, achievement, satisfaction, new projects, the excitement of future successes, and he may be frank enough to mention that he enjoys receiving the respect and praise of others.

If you praise people's actions, you encourage more of the right behaviour and a basic desire to do the right thing and receive more praise. This is so obviously true that one wonders why so many managers spend more of their time criticizing people than they do praising them. Perhaps they feel surrounded by daily challenges and problems so that they notice all the errors and things that go wrong. They feel that if things go wrong because people have slipped up, they must point out the mistake or the mistake will be repeated, and therefore they have no alternative but to criticize poor performance.

Yes, that's true, but it is also a potential trap for managers. If it appears to your team that every time they try it leads to criticism from you, they will soon learn to avoid trying. A symptom of this condition would be when you notice how some team members have developed strategies to look busy while actually avoiding doing things that might lead to criticism.

Check your language. Just to be sure, for one day, keep count of the praises and the criticisms that you issue. If you give more criticism than praise, people will discount the praise. The mass of people are super-sensitive to criticism. One ounce of criticism weighs heavier on them than pounds of praise. For this reason, your count should reveal a ratio of at least four to one in favour of praising.

When you must criticize, be careful to censure the action rather than the person: 'What you just did was bad' rather than 'You are bad'. The first framing of words suggests that the person made a mistake and should try not to repeat it, whereas saying 'You are bad' attacks a person's sense of worth and simply alienates them because they feel that you have unjustly criticized their core being.

A final important point: if you repeatedly tell people that they are good you may breed a smug and arrogant team, which would create a different set of problems for you. Avoid this by being specific. Praise actions and consequential outcomes. Tell people why the action they took was good. Tell them briefly, in public, and move on. You will notice that other team members look up and take note, so that praising one person will encourage several.

*'To say "well done" to any bit of good work is to take hold of the powers which have made the effort and strengthen them beyond our knowledge.'*

*Phillips Brooks, 1835–1893,*
*American clergyman, author*
*and Bishop of Massachusetts*

# Law 12

## Managers tend to flog
## their willing horses to exhaustion

Some horses are so willing that when the rider or coach driver whips them on, the horse responds by working until it drops, literally collapsing from exhaustion. A few horses are so extremely willing that they require being held back at all times; otherwise, incapable of pacing their effort, they would quickly become worn out and useless. Some people are like this. They don't physically collapse on the floor, but the results can be equally dramatic.

Do you have any willing horses in your team? If so, you're very fortunate. They will work hard and get through more work than other people do. And they set an excellent example. But beware: if you push them too far, they will show little sign of nearing exhaustion, until the day that you find your valued asset is suddenly making uncharacteristic mistakes, or is extremely irritable, or is unaccountably aggressive, or even worse, is at home suffering from mental and physical exhaustion, perhaps even work-related stress.

Willing horses have some very endearing qualities. For example, they will probably never say, '*I can't cope with any more work.*' Also, once they understand what you want, and provided they know how to do the job, they will need little or no further supervision. You give them the work and the work gets done. You give them yet more work and, unlike some others in your team, they accept it without question and work even harder! You feel you can rely on them. They make your life easier. They are star performers.

Having identified a willing horse, you need to know just how much work they are able to cope with. There seems to be no point in under-loading them, so when do you stop piling on the work?

They react to extra work by trying to cope. They can be seen, heads down, hard at it for every minute of the day. Then, when this is not enough, they try working longer hours or taking work home. This should ring warning bells for you. They won't admit to you that they're not coping, because that's not in their nature. And if you're not looking, you'll fail to notice how they start spiralling out of control.

Feeling under extreme pressure, they doggedly press on, but now they start to make the odd mistake. They appear a little forgetful (unusual for them) and the standard of work drops a little. At this point, many managers notice a drop in performance and react with a telling-off or criticism. The willing horse thinks, *'Ouch! That hurts! Unjustified! I'm working like crazy here.'*

Next, they notice that co-workers have a comparatively easy time, with less to do, more time for the occasional social chat and more time for lunch. Others work fewer hours yet receive equal praise and probably equal pay. The willing horse becomes a little irritable, perhaps even rebellious. And finally, the chain of events comes to the inevitable end. He or she chooses to leave, or becomes genuinely ill, or is dismissed for rebellious behaviour. A great asset has been lost.

The inexperienced manager may not realize what caused his best worker to turn sour. And a stupid manager may realize that he pushed this person too far, but wrongly believe that people are expendable. That would be very foolish because willing horses are a rare asset. They're invaluable not only because they get so much work done, but also because they set an example that lifts the performance of the entire team.

Consider the skilful coachman. With a team of four or more horses, the expert coachman will place his most willing horse up front, to set the pace, to show an example and inspire the rest of the team to give their best. However, the skilled coachman will occasionally rein in his team and pace his willing horse, to ensure that his prize asset remains capable of giving its best year after year.

Identify your willing horses; look for signs of them becoming exhausted and help them to pace themselves. They'll probably deny that there is anything wrong. That's another feature of a willing horse. Despite their protests and denials, make sure they take a break when necessary to recharge their batteries and refresh themselves. That way, they can remain among your most valuable people assets.

*'It's the willing horse they saddle the most.'*

*Anonymous Jamaican proverb,*
*referring to the treatment of slaves*

# Law 13

## People easily become addicted
## to being a firefighter

Is it wise to be the hero of the day who tackles yet another mammoth and immediate problem and earns the reputation of being a great firefighter?

If you, or one of your team members, are an inveterate firefighter, you must beware of the consequences. There is a crucial difference between making quick decisions, acting decisively, and being a firefighter.

People who have a reputation for frequently rescuing the organization from impending disaster acquire a certain kudos. Organizations have a tendency to reward these people by giving them ever larger and more urgent problems to tackle. This serves to create a live-for-the-day firefighting culture, which can be extremely counterproductive.

Being an accomplished firefighter feels intensely satisfying too. Look back to the last time you successfully averted impending disaster. The adrenaline pumped, giving you a real buzz as you reacted to the challenge and saved the day.

Ultimately, you will severely limit your achievements if you are always reactive rather than proactive. You could not work on your high-return activities or your pre-planned high priorities. You are stuck in living for today instead of building a better future. Furthermore, if you fight enough fires, the law of averages dictates that eventually you will get burnt. One day, you won't be able to solve the problem and the consequences could be serious for you.

Recovering from being in a firefighting situation is not easy, but these ideas should help:

- Earmark a slice of your time for seizing control. If necessary, hide away for a while, so that you can plan your way out of trouble
- Search for ways to do it right first time. Many of today's problems are the results of yesterday's botched jobs. Take action to prevent the same problem recurring
- Very often, the problem that you see is the result of an action several links back in a chain of events. Dig deep until you identify the root causes for the crisis
- Don't automatically accept first and obvious solutions; there may be better and more permanent ones. New and different solutions to old problems frequently lead to inventing new ideas that form the foundations upon which you can build major successes
- Make sure that nobody in your team is an inveterate firefighter, hooked on the adrenaline and reluctant to kick the habit!
- Take heart, because firefighting is a symptom of a problem. A problem is a symptom of an opportunity. Find the solution to the problem and you may well unearth the opportunity

*'The significant problems cannot be solved at the same level of thinking we were at when we created them . . . In the middle of every difficulty lies opportunity.'*

*Albert Einstein, 1879–1955,*
*German physicist, best known for his theories of*
*Relativity and Mass-energy Equivalence (E=mc$^2$)*

# Law 14

## Attention seekers never change

We all have a deep-seated need for attention. For most of us, hearing an occasional *'Well done'* satisfies our need; but a small percentage of us demand much, much more attention.

Some children receive overwhelming and constant attention from their doting parents. As a result, they have been conditioned for life. They expect to always be the centre of attention, if not they feel something is wrong. People like this cannot cope with life unless they are the centre of interest at all times.

When you were at school, you may have noticed that a few of the children worked at grabbing the majority of the teacher's attention. They were even prepared to get into trouble just to be noticed; they revelled in the attention they consequently received. They would rather suffer a scolding than be ignored.

Children that become hooked on receiving constant attention carry this deep-rooted need into adulthood. By the time they arrive in your team, they could have many years' experience in how to manipulate their colleagues and their supervisor – namely you! They will almost certainly have more expertise in getting their own way than you will have in coping with such a demanding person.

Here are some of the signs: devoting time to charming others in order to receive frequent compliments and admiration in return; fishing for constant attention; expecting other team members to defer to them; a lack of sensitivity towards other team members; and even encouraging romantic or sexual relationships to enable them to get their own way. Their first objective is not to get the job done but to get attention. This type of person is extremely disruptive, the absolute opposite of a team player.

Fortunately, only a small percentage of people fall into this category, maybe one in a hundred, but if one member of your team is continually striving for a great deal of your time, beware. If you further discover that when you don't immediately respond to this person they start causing trouble for you, then you have an attention seeker in your midst. If so, the bad news is that things are not going to get better.

Soon, other members of the team will feel they are not getting a fair share of your attention. Worse still, you will find everyone diverts focus from achieving the objectives to competing for extra recognition of their needs. Disagreements between team members follow, and the real culprit, the attention seeker, will expertly appear not to be the cause.

The attention seeker is not going to change a lifetime habit. One tactic that you can employ is to load more work on to the attention seeker so that he or she doesn't have time to make trouble. But if this does not work, your final recourse is unpalatable but inevitable. Eventually, he or she will have to go, or you and the team are going to suffer.

*'Excessive attention, even if it's negative, is such a powerful "reward" to a child that it actually reinforces the undesirable behavior.'*

*Stanley Turecki, American psychiatrist, from his book* The Difficult Child

# Law 15

## People prefer to leave
## the nasty jobs until last

Nobody relishes the prospect of calling a customer to give him the bad news that his order is going to be delivered late. Nobody relishes the prospect of reprimanding an employee. And who will want to rush to the boss and admit they've just committed an expensive blunder? We think, *'I must just do so-and-so first,'* delaying the nasty job until later. But this has downsides.

When we delay an unpleasant task, we suffer a gnawing guilt that eats away at our enjoyment of life and makes us less able to do our job. And as time passes, most problems escalate in magnitude until they become bigger issues that are even more difficult to resolve.

As manager, you need to know about the minor gaffes as soon as possible, before they get worse. You want to limit the damage as early as possible, and herein lies the dilemma.

If, when people make a mistake, you treat them too lightly, then you encourage them to feel that you don't care too much about high standards. If you come down too hard on the person who gets it wrong, then people will go to great lengths to hide away their slip-ups where you can't find them.

If you treat people harshly and they feel crushed, you take away all of their confidence, so that in future they won't feel confident enough to take decisions upon themselves. This leads to you needing to approve, in advance, everything that is done. You become so overburdened with tiny and inconsequential decisions that you have no time left for things of importance.

Your solutions are:

- Tell people that the longer they put off informing you about a problem, the stronger will be the reprimand
- Turn every mistake into a learning experience, where you invest the cost of the problem in teaching your team how to do it right next time
- Be philosophical about mistakes, so people know that you accept the reality that everyone drops the ball from time to time. Don't wail and moan, but immediately after you have delivered a short reprimand, pragmatically move on to finding the solution
- Accept ultimate responsibility, and carry the can for mistakes made by your team. You will find that they will respect you for this and respond by trying harder for you
- If people repeat a mistake, make your reprimand more severe, and if they make the same mistake for a third time, you must come down hard. If, after that, they still repeat the mistake, then you must discover why this keeps happening. You must find a solution to ensure it won't happen again

- Finally, instill the tradition that you always get nasty jobs over and done with so that, with no lingering guilt, you can invest the remainder of the day in more positive, productive and pleasant activity

---

*'Actions feed and strengthen confidence; inaction in all forms feeds fear. To fight fear, act. To increase fear – wait, put off, postpone.'*

*David Joseph Schwartz,*
*author of* The Magic of Thinking Big

---

# Law 16

## People want to be given their work in one of only four ways

It's a strange thing, but often people just won't do what you want, merely because they don't approve of the way you asked; they didn't like the way you delegated the work.

On these occasions, they are unlikely to share with you the real reason for their lack of progress. You may be mystified, thinking *'Why aren't they getting on with their work'* or *'Why are they making such a poor job of this?'*

An age-old solution to this situation was to crack the whip. We don't do that now, but when faced with low performance, many bosses' first reaction is to apply pressure when the root cause was that they created resistance by not delegating the work effectively.

We'll get more done if we adjust our delegation style to suit the person and the situation. To complicate the issue, as managers we each have one natural preferred style of delegating that suits our own personality. Naturally, without thinking, we tend to use this style the most.

Likewise, employees each have a preferred delegation style for receiving work. When the preferred styles of manager and employee mismatch, the problems start.

People prefer to receive instructions in one of four distinctly different ways:

- 'Just tell me straight exactly what you want me to do'
- 'I want you to consider my opinion before you decide what I am going to do'
- 'I feel a need to be the one who decides what I'm going to do'
- 'I want all the team to discuss this and come to a joint decision, and after that I'll be happy to do it'

Consider each preference.

*'Just tell me straight exactly what you want me to do.'*

There are people who always work best when simply told what to do. They may need support along the way, or they may work best when left alone to get on with the job. Frequently the people who prefer this delegation style are good at doing repetitive work to a high standard. Usually, this type of person will tell their manager how they prefer to receive work, which may often include receiving written instructions. And often these people will maintain interest over time, even with repetitive work that others would find boring.

*'I want you to consider my opinion before you decide what I am going to do.'*

Some people just cannot commit wholeheartedly to any task or to achieving any objective until the manager has first shown that he or she values their opinion. Often these prove to be the creative people who are good at finding new solutions to problems, or new and better ways of doing things.

*'I feel a need to be the one who decides what I'm going to do.'*

A few people have real trouble with accepting orders, period. These people have problems with doing anything delegated to them by others. They need to feel totally in control of how they spend their lives at work. You may think you should avoid having people like this in your team. However, often these are the very people who achieve great things for you with little or no supervision. But first, you must help them become committed to achieving your objectives. You do this by investing time in presenting the objectives. They allow you to control the objectives in return for you taking a little time to convince them, plus giving them freedom to control their own minutes and hours. However, you still need to review their progress from time to time, and to make sure they don't drift off track from your objective.

*'I want all the team to discuss this and to come to a joint decision, and after that I'll be happy to do it.'*

There are also employees who crave a democracy at work. They want to have their say. They can see the advantage of ensuring that the whole team agrees. They like the committee process. Often, they are committed to achieving things for the team success, the common good, but find themselves rebelling against anything that smacks of dictatorship at work.

Very few companies, if any, attempt to run their

business as a democracy, so you might think these employees are destined to a future of unemployment. But these people may also be the ones who care the most about their work mates. They will nurture their fellow workers during the tough times and play an important role in building the team spirit that is so essential for achieving prolonged success. You help them to accept your decisions and your delegation by allowing them some freedom to speak, by listening to their contribution and by acknowledging the value of their contribution.

This picture of four different types of people illustrates that everyone contributes individual strengths to a team, and the method you use to hand out the work can either motivate them to do their best or inadvertently create unnecessary barriers to performance.

Consider the members of your team: what style of delegation do you think each person prefers? If you don't know the answers, observation will provide the clues.

We also need to vary our approach to suit each different set of circumstances. If the building were on fire we would not hesitate; we'd simply tell people what to do in a loud and commanding voice. This is definitely not a time for considering a person's preferred delegation style, neither is there time for any discussion. That demanding approach is usually correct for the *act now or the problem gets worse* type of business emergency.

But on other occasions, you need to use different

strokes for different folks. Being aware of the four styles and pausing to think which is most appropriate to the person and the situation quickly enables a manager to become skilled at choosing the right approach. Always pause and decide which style is appropriate for the occasion:

- You tell him or her exactly what you want done, explaining clearly the appropriate who, how, what, why and when details. Or . . .
- Consult with him or her, asking their opinion while retaining the right to decide what they will actually do. Or . . .
- Explain what you need to achieve, what you want them to do to help you achieve the goal, allowing them to say, *'Yes, I'll do that.'* And if they avoid committing, or say *'No'*, then you take time to find out why and address the reasons. Or . . .
- You involve the full team in deciding how you will achieve the objectives, what tasks will be completed and who will do the work and take responsibility for the completion of each task. When deciding to use this democratic approach, be careful that it really is the best method for the occasion. Also, be aware that afterwards, if you are not pleased with the group decision and you suddenly switch to a very hands-on dictatorial management style, your team will feel at best confused and at worst that you have ignored them, which creates resentment

Unfortunately, most managers press on, forever in a rush, without pausing to think for a moment about exactly what they are doing.

*'There is no expedient to which a man will not go to avoid the real labor of thinking.'*

*Thomas Edison, 1847–1931,*
*American inventor and businessman*

# Law 17
## Productivity is a natural trait

Contrary to the belief of many world-weary managers, we are all naturally productive people. Productivity is an in-built human trait that we all switch on when circumstances are right for us.

To unleash our natural productive ability we need:

- To know the goals and to visualize what success will look and feel like
- To feel confident that we are progressing towards achieving the goals
- To focus our attention on working towards achieving the goals, discarding irrelevant or minor tasks in favour of goal-directed work

Any manager who works on creating the three conditions above will see team performance lift. It's not about frenetic activity and rush. This only leads to exhaustion and mistakes.

Create productive circumstances by ensuring that your people know and understand the goals. Encourage them to enjoy the upcoming feeling of success when they achieve each goal. No matter what has gone before, encourage people to engage in productive goal-directed activity right now, for the remainder of the current hour and for what is left of today. Be unconcerned about past wasted time.

Invest time wisely – starting right now.

Every day, allocate part of your time to encouraging your team to invest their own time in activities that lead to results, rather than merely to spend it in busy work. And be sure that you set a good example. Show that personal productivity is important to you by investing your own hours effectively.

And be sure to reward the productive efforts of team members. Many managers overlook this, focusing instead on rewarding only attainment. Productive effort is equally praiseworthy, because it inevitably leads to good results.

> 'Productivity is a trait we're born with, it's not an acquired skill.'
>
> *Richard Ott,*
> *co-author of* Unleashing Productivity

# Law 18

# People are easily tricked into thinking that urgent equals important

There are *important* tasks and *urgent* tasks. Very, very few tasks are both urgent and important!

In working life, the words urgent and important tend to be poles apart, constantly competing for your attention and tugging you in opposite directions. For example, at some time most managers are required to produce, or contribute to, a major plan. It could be the plan for next year or a major project. Or, it could be that you need to give careful thought to exactly how your team is going to achieve the objectives for the coming month.

Such major issues require careful thought: how should you organize the people and the work; what needs to be done first; can you meet the standards required; is your team trying to achieve the impossible; do you have sufficient resources in people, money, technology, etc.?

Planning is of crucial importance. Getting the plan wrong could have serious consequences. Getting it right could lead to major success. Yet, typically, managers delay their planning sessions while the minor but urgent tasks of the day take precedence. Eventually, when they can no longer delay, they rush through the preparation of an important plan and foolishly set their ill-conceived plans into concrete, as immovable targets which they strive to achieve, beaten by inadequate planning before they started. Important has become the victim of urgent.

Every member of your team needs to decide between urgent and important tasks on a daily basis. For example, someone calls to remind a member of your team that he or she needs a response to a request for information made yesterday. Naturally, your team member feels the urgency created by the caller's persistence. They want to help but they have difficulty fitting in the request while completing the important assignment that you have delegated to them. The team member tries to find the time to respond, and after receiving a couple more verbal chasings, they halt work on your important job and devote an hour to collecting the information required. But supplying that information was less important than the lost work on your project. One hour has now been spent on a task that had little or nothing to do with the team's responsibilities or objective. Our desire to help co-workers is one example of a frequent urgent-versus-important trap. You may find yourself doing someone else's job for them, while part of your own job remains untouched.

Of course, you will always have your share of minor yet urgent jobs. But if you do the minor tasks first, the chances are that your day will pass quickly by, with your top priority remaining untouched, or at best only part completed. At the end of the day, you feel tired from all your effort combined with the frustration of making inadequate progress on the most important job.

When you ensure that the urgent events of the day do not control the entire work agenda, you free up more time for major and important tasks. How can you achieve that?

There is no simple list of rules that, if followed, will always guarantee the correct balance between urgency and importance. This area of managing yourself and your subordinates is an art, but here are some proven tactics:

- Be ruthless about working on your top priorities throughout most of the day. Be uncompromising when it comes to decisions about how you invest time
- Instead of starting the day by clearing your desk of the minor tasks, sweep these aside until later. Start working on the big issues, and progress them as far as possible. Then, having made some satisfying progress, leave just enough time for dealing with the trivia in one hectic and intensely productive session
- Many people believe that if they are aggressive, persistent and demanding they can elevate their own priorities to the top of your pile of work. Don't be fooled by low priorities arriving in disguise
- You will fail to do some things. It is in the very nature of work that there will never be enough

time available in which to do it all. Therefore, prioritize your work, so that you attend to the most important jobs first. That way, you will fail to achieve the least important things, rather than fail to achieve the most important things

- Teach your team how to decide between urgent tasks and important tasks. Give them guidelines on how you want them to decide what to do, and what not to do. Teach them how to invest their minutes and hours in each day. You don't want them to refer to you every time a new task arrives. Instead, you want to teach them how to make the judgements that you would approve of

*'Things which matter most must never be at the mercy of things which matter least.'*

*Johann Wolfgang von Goethe*

# Law 19

# Most people hate being organized

*'An untidy desk is a sign of genius. It might look a mess to you, but I can put my hand on any document, immediately.'* Problem: what happens when this employee is off sick and you need to find some essential information in a hurry?

It does not matter whether or not this employee is capable of working efficiently despite the mess, which is extremely unlikely, because the personal organization of each team member has to conform to some basic norms of good practice, or the team will suffer.

And when you show that important visitor around, what will he or she think of you and your team, as they survey the mess and apparent chaos?

You all need to conform to some common standards of personal organization, and collectively among your team there must be an efficient flow of work, documents, etc. And there must be easy access to information about work in progress and historical data that may prove useful.

And these disciplines must include the organization of information held on computers, both organization-wide systems and personal computers. If people fail to organize their emails and other files on their computer, their productivity must surely take a dive. Employees who use personal computers at work must accept that they are the custodians of essential information belonging to the organization, which needs to be available if required by others at times when the user of the computer is not around.

Some employees fight tooth and nail to preserve what they perceive as their personal right to remain disorganized or to operate some personal organization system that only they can understand. They may even feel that having a unique and unfathomable method of working helps to make them indispensable. You can't allow this because, eventually, the team will suffer. This person's attitude will create problems for the team and for you personally. Being organized is not an option; it is a prime responsibility for every manager to ensure that the flow of documents through his or her team is well organized, universally understood and easily accessible.

The best administrative systems and disciplines are as simple as possible and save time, rather than creating an additional workload. You need to design systems that make life easier for your team. If you personally don't know how to do that, enlist expert outside help – and quickly!

*'I have never met a successful person in any field of endeavour who was not well organized.'*

*Mark H. McCormack, 1930–2003,*
*founder of International Management Group*

# Law 20

## Managers tend to give the worst tasks to their best people

It's a challenge. To whom will you delegate the most difficult tasks?

Consider this situation. Your team has a number of different objectives to achieve. You divide the objectives into a number of tasks and you allocate one to each team member. Some of these tasks require dealing with people outside the team, probably including a mix of clients or customers, and other departments or suppliers.

One of the tasks is especially difficult, because it requires liaising with a notoriously difficult and uncooperative person. This person frequently complains without cause, habitually asks for preferential treatment, demands an unreasonable level of service and yet fails to be consistent at keeping their own promises. Furthermore, when successfully completed, this one task will contribute only a small amount to the overall success of your team. But it must be done.

Your most experienced team member is very capable at handling difficult people. Would you allocate the task to him or her? Most managers would do so. It seems the obvious solution. But it may be unwise.

Most managers automatically match high levels of skill with high levels of difficulty, and in doing so they often limit the overall achievement of their team. There is no automatic correlation between high difficulty and high returns. Just because a task is difficult, it does not mean it will yield big results, profit, achievement, etc. Experience suggests that, perversely, quite the reverse is often true: the most awkward jobs, when completed, deliver the lowest return for time and effort invested.

If you want the easy life, target your best people at avoiding problems and divide the remaining jobs between the other team members. That way, you'll find fewer problems reach your desk, but you won't achieve much. And in the end, managers are rated according to the results of their team, so before deciding to whom to delegate any difficult task, the shrewd manager pauses to ask these questions:

- Who will do it best?
- Who will do it quickest?
- Who will do it with the least management support required from me?
- If I give the job to so-and-so, will there be a downside to this? In particular, what will be the overall effect upon team results?
- Which match of people to tasks will deliver the highest performance for my team?

The answers to those five questions will help you come to the most balanced judgement. Whenever possible, you want to avoid having your best people tied up all day coping with the most taxing stuff and achieving little. More will be achieved if you let your best people loose on the objectives that bring the highest rewards, where the team's overall results may skyrocket.

For the highest possible results, always target your best people at the biggest opportunities.

> 'It may be necessary to go South for a while, in order to journey North.'
>
> Edward de Bono, b.1933,
> originator of the term 'lateral thinking'

# Law 21

## Some unintelligent people are a great asset, but others are dangerous

James is not the smartest member of the team; in fact, he can be a bit slow on the uptake. But despite this, James is a valuable team player. Every day, without fail, he performs the same essential routines that are necessary to keep the department functioning.

Others would find his job dull; the repetitive nature of the work would lead them to become frustrated and bored. And bored people tend to let their minds wander to more exciting lines of thought, and then their low degree of concentration leads to mistakes and slapdash work. Not James, though. He is satisfied with his role and delivers reliable work. He needs close supervision when asked to do something out of his familiar routine, but otherwise he can be left to his own devices. Thus, James is a great asset while doing his current job.

Like James, Eva is not too smart. However, she is a hard-working contributor to the team. Eva is also confident and ambitious. Having been a member of the team for two years now, she has considerable knowledge about how things work. In view of all these qualities, it seems sensible to promote Eva and make her the person responsible for looking after the big new contract. The fresh challenge will revitalize Eva's enthusiasm and her knowledge will help her do well. However, Eva's enthusiasm, knowledge and ambition outstrip her intellect. Does this matter? Well, that depends on her degree of autonomy and the challenges ahead. First, consider these thoughts about intelligence and work.

One well-known measure of a person's intelligence is the IQ Test, which involves mental gymnastics using spatial, mathematical and verbal reasoning. The test is performed against the clock, and the calculated results are compared with the results of other people of similar age. Thus, your IQ is a measure of your ability to reason through a series of number, word, pictorial and space-related puzzles. These four aspects of reasoning cover almost all decisions made at work.

*The American Heritage Dictionary* defines intelligence like this: 'intelligent usually implies the ability to cope with new problems and to use the power of reasoning and inference effectively.' At work, using reasoning involves decisions followed by actions.

Now let's return to Eva. Her undoubted knowledge and enthusiasm should enable her to cope with the greater part of her extra responsibilities. However, when it comes to making decisions that affect the success of the big new contract, her limited ability to think through the consequences of potential financial changes (maths reasoning), or to fully understand and interpret other people's meaning (verbal reasoning) may trip her up. She may well make poor decisions with problematic or costly repercussions. Thus, Eva could be a dangerous choice.

- Less intelligent people are often ideally suited to work that others would find repetitive and boring. With careful supervision, they are therefore a great asset in some essential roles
- Less intelligent people who are ambitious and confident usually become dangerous to your success when they attain decision-making roles

If you have a person in your team who is a little dumb in some vital respects, you need to recognize the limitations in his or her ability to make good decisions. You must take care to think through in advance exactly how much freedom to allow them.

Ensure they know on which occasions you want them to *'Just keep me informed'*, when you need them to *'Check your decision with me before you take action'*, and when they should *'Refer to me before you decide'*. And always be careful to treat them with respect.

> *'To be considered stupid and to be told so is more painful than being called gluttonous, mendacious, violent, lascivious, lazy, cowardly: every weakness, every vice, has found its defenders, its rhetoric, its ennoblement and exaltation, but stupidity hasn't.'*
>
> *Primo Levi, 1919–1987,*
> *Italian chemist and author*

# Law 22

## Some lazy people are a great asset, but others must go

Among the employees of every organization there are some people who are just plain lazy by nature. You may feel the temptation to immediately get rid of these people, but wait – consider this first.

There are three types of lazy people at work:

Type 1: *'I'm lazy because I couldn't give a damn. My main goal at work is to get through the day while expending as little effort as possible. I'm an expert in work avoidance. I've been like this all my life and I am not going to change!'*

Type 2: *'I'm lazy because I'm bored. So far nothing has happened at work that has motivated me to get off my butt and get active.'*

Type 3: *'I'm lazy because I want the rewards, without having to work for them. I find the easy option that gets me what I want without me personally having to make much effort.'*

With a little luck, your lazy team member might be of Type 2. These people have often become lazy because they found their job too easy. It quickly became boring. Then, as enthusiasm slowly ebbed away, they started to switch off and now they plod along doing the minimum. They may occasionally relieve their boredom by bemoaning their lot and criticizing. The laziness and disaffection that you see is the outcome. Before you give up on this person, it would be wise to give them a second chance. Perhaps they have a talented brain that is dramatically underutilized.

If you can find a role or task that presents an interesting mental challenge, it may shake them out of their apathy as their rise to the challenge. It's worth trying. You need to learn whether this person is temporarily lazy or permanently so. The best outcome is that they turn out to have been stricken by temporary laziness.

However, if you discover this person is permanently lazy, it is unlikely that you will ever find a suitable role for them. Worse still, a lazy person will drag down the performance of those around them. And they may occasionally fail to do something, which severely damages the team's results.

In these circumstances, there may be no other alternative but for you to protect your team by moving the problem person out of your team as quickly as possible.

Some people fall into Type 3. They are lazy, but they remain focused on achievement. It's just that they want others to do the work while they enjoy the easy life.

Actually, many high achievers are like this. Being intelligent, they think up good ways to accomplish things. Being lazy, they look for easy ways to have other people do the work for them, while they personally sit back and relax, which gives them more time to think. Not a bad strategy when you consider it; laziness can have its virtues!

So, your strategy is:

Type 1: Get rid of him or her.

Type 2: Test with an interesting new challenge.

Type 3: Look for ways to harness and to capitalize upon this person's thinking skills.

The good manager is prepared to be tough and move or remove lazy people when necessary, but only reluctantly and after testing to see if a great performance lies un-awakened.

---

*'Whenever there is a hard job to be done I assign it to a lazy man; he is sure to find an easy way of doing it.'*

*Walter Chrysler, 1875–1940,*
*founder of the Chrysler Corporation*

---

# Law 23

## Most people say NO in code

Sometimes we know that we can't achieve what our manager wants. It is a fact of working life that there is not enough time for people to say yes to every request. Occasionally, we all have to say no.

Rather than simply saying 'No', people often want to impart the bad news gently, out of consideration for the feelings of others. They attempt to soften the blow and convey their hard message without causing any unnecessary upset.

Others can't face the potential conflict that might result when they say 'No' to their manager, so instead they use a form of words that half conveys their meaning and hopefully avoids any potential clash.

The words they choose are so soft that the meaning often goes unnoticed. As a manager, you will often be on the receiving end of this tactical talk. For example . . .

When someone should be upfront and tell you 'No, I'm sorry, but I can't do that', they may instead say 'I'll try' or 'It should be possible' or 'I'll do my best'. Later, when you remind these people of their commitment, they may respond with something like 'I'll get round to it soon' or 'Leave it with me' or 'I'll get back to you'.

These euphemistic and non-committal phrases are all soft words to disguise the hard and unpalatable fact that they already know they are going to let you down, but don't feel too good about openly admitting it. In code, they are really saying, *'I'd like to help but I can't, and I want to avoid telling you straight.'*

We all respect the people we can trust to deliver on promises. The people in your team that you can truly rely on are undoubtedly also the ones who have the guts to say no when it is the honest response. Next time you delegate a task, listen carefully to the words used in response. If you receive a form of words that could be interpreted as avoiding commitment, be aware that later you may find that the task remains incomplete.

If you are in doubt, question the person carefully. Ask how they will prioritize this new task. How will they fit this extra work into their schedule? Check that the person has all the resources necessary to complete the job for you. Double-check the commitment whenever someone avoids giving a plain yes or no.

And instill into your people the ethic that, even if it means giving you bad news, you expect frank, honest and sincere answers to your questions.

> *'Sincerity is impossible, unless it pervades the whole being, and the pretence of it saps the very foundation of character.'*
>
> James Russell Lowell, 1819–1891,
> American poet, editor and diplomat

# Law 24
# Work expands to fill the time available
## (*Parkinson's Law*)

How many people do you know who go home at the end of the day having first relaxed for a few minutes, because they have managed to complete every task for that day? Very few, I expect. The majority of people go home leaving piles of unfinished work carried forward to the following day.

Often, it appears, there will never be enough time for everything that needs to be done. This can be dreadfully depressing. We feel as if we are running on a never-ending treadmill. There is no single, easy solution to this dilemma, but when you recognize the problem, you can make a start at doing something about it.

When you accept that you will never be able to do everything, this means you accept that some jobs will never be done. This is reality. Therefore, we must choose carefully what we will fail to do. We must fail to do the least important things, but do the most important things without fail.

Try this approach. Arrive for work a little earlier than usual so that you can have about 15 minutes alone before starting the events of the day. First, quickly decide if there are any extremely important items that you must respond to immediately. Put aside the rest until later. Resist the temptation to start the day by replying to all your voicemails, answering all the emails and clearing your desk of all the small stuff.

Next, prioritize your list for the day. Be tough. Pick the low-grade, low-return activities and relegate them to the end of your list. Choose the high-grade, high-return activities and promote them to the top of your list. Work on these first. Succeed in progressing them, while you fail to do the trivia. Feel comfortable with delaying all the small stuff. Be determined to do the important stuff properly.

Continue this way for as long as possible. Allow a period at the end of the day for batch-processing all the small stuff – the emails, the voicemails and the various notes you have written yourself over the course of the day. Make this a compressed period of activity. Imagine you are leaving on vacation at the end of the day and approach your work accordingly. You have no choice but to complete, to delegate or to trash the least important.

When the inevitable happens, and you go home at the end of the day leaving some trivial work untouched, you will have the satisfaction of knowing that you have invested your time in the most important, high-return activities.

This is the method used by many of the highest performers in business. When you have proved to yourself that it works, and that you are now completing more important work than ever before, teach your people how to prioritize their work, helping them use good judgement in ordering their daily list.

When your team has become good at prioritizing their work, you can feel confident in empowering them to make many more decisions without referring to you, which will lift the overall productivity of the team still higher.

You must be ruthless about ignoring trivia in order to make time for what matters most. And you must delegate whenever possible. You want your team to make all decisions at the lowest practical link in the chain of command, because when you prevent people from doing work of consequence they respond by busying themselves with other stuff. Soon they have filled their day brim full so that they feel they are making an important contribution, thus proving the ever-present essential truth that work tends to expand to fill the time available, plus a little extra.

*'The man who is denied the opportunity of taking decisions of importance begins to regard as important the decisions he is allowed to take. He becomes fussy about filing, keen on seeing the pencils are sharpened, eager to ensure the windows are opened (or shut) and apt to use two or three different coloured pens.'*

*C. Northcote Parkinson, 1909–1993, British naval historian who coined Parkinson's Law*

# Law 25

## People tend to do things at the accepted time, which is often not the effective time

Work patterns, like society, direct us to follow the crowd and live to the norm. If you rebel and do things your way, people brand you as an eccentric. For example, most of us work from Monday to Friday, and then fight the crowds to do our shopping on a Saturday, when the shops are at their busiest.

On Sunday, many of us swarm to the same get-away-from-it-all spot. We crowd together at the beach, or along beautiful forest walks, when what we really seek is the solitude and space to be found when you visit mid-week, when other people are at work.

The most effective people resist going with the flow, they tend to be a little unconventional. Let's take one extreme to illustrate how different things can be. When you hear a bestselling author interviewed on the radio, you often learn that their normal routine is to work from 6 a.m. until 11 a.m., and then break for an enjoyable afternoon walk, followed by an early dinner and a return to the job at 7 p.m. for a couple more hours. Other authors just work until they drop, and then take a vacation to recuperate! They choose to work at the most effective time for their pattern of energy.

The author who works from home obviously enjoys a flexibility that is not available to most of us. But we do have some leeway. For example, consider these examples of the most effective prime times for doing things.

The prime time for banking cash takings is when the line at the bank is at its shortest, not when everyone else visits the bank.

The busy executive generally arrives in the office before everyone else. His or her daily schedule of appointments probably starts around the usual time of 9 a.m. If you want to speak with senior executives personally, you'll find the prime time to call them is very, very early in the day, when most people are battling the commute, or still in bed.

The prime time for concentrating on your planning is when you can be sure of no interruptions. The usual working hours are when you receive the most interruptions. This means that you work extra long hours, either starting early or working late – or how about considering being a little unconventional? For instance, why not lock yourself away for a while, or even take to the hills where the view is inspirational and the solitary peace helps you concentrate?

Naturally, you cannot choose to service your customers when they are not at work. And you need to be available when the boss wants you. You can't change this type of demand, but you can get away with making your team a little eccentric about the time you choose to get many jobs done, and in the process dramatically improve team productivity.

Study the tasks completed by your team, looking for opportunities to break the mould and reallocate jobs to a time or place when they will be done better, quicker or with less hassle. Whenever possible, move jobs to their most effective time and then re-invest the time saved in extra productivity.

*'The best leaders are apt to be found among those executives who have a strong component of unorthodoxy in their characters. Instead of resisting innovation, they symbolize it – and companies cannot grow without innovation.'*

*David Ogilvy, 1911–1999,*
*founder of Ogilvy & Mather,*
*often called 'The Father of Advertising'*

# Law 26

## When leaders don't create the culture they want, they get a culture that they definitely don't want

Every organization has a culture. This culture characterizes the traditions, customs and way of life for the people who work in the organization. And within the organization, every team has its individual culture. This law creates a marvellous opportunity for every team leader, plus a challenge that must be conquered.

Without intervention, your team culture will gravitate towards being non-productive. This is a depressing reality of life at work. It happens because the majority of people prefer what they see as the easy life.

Most people want to work within their comfort zone, rather than step outside it and extend themselves a little. They prefer things to be comfortable and as effortless as possible, whereas the team leader should feel the need to push for extra accomplishment.

Obviously, you, the leader, are a minority of one. Therefore, you must take positive action to create the productive and effective culture you need. If not, your team will gravitate towards a more easy-going life. Consequently, you need to 1) define, 2) vocalize and 3) indoctrinate, through repetition, the culture that you need.

One effective way for you to embed a new culture is for you to promote appropriate 'We do it like this . . .' statements. Consider these 'we' statements:

*'We always answer the phone within three rings.'*
*'We always answer the phone cheerfully.'*
*'If we know we cannot do it, we say so honestly.'*
*'We do it right first time.'*

Affirmations like these are not pop psychology, but one method by which, consciously or unconsciously, teams of people have always bonded together. All people feel a surge of family and belonging when they identify with a group of others who share common beliefs and objectives.

Make sure that you frequently voice suitable 'we' statements and then listen out for what follows. Before very long, you will hear a breakthrough. One day, you will start to hear members of your team repeating your words to others: *'In this team, we do it like this . . .'* Other manifestations of group culture shortly follow, such as feelings of belonging, pride in common beliefs, team loyalty, supporting each other and a desire to achieve things together.

---

*'We are what we repeatedly do. Excellence, then, is not an act, but a habit.'*

*Aristotle, 384–322 BC,*
*Greek philosopher, student of Plato,*
*teacher of Alexander the Great*

---

## Law 27

## When the manager lacks
## self-discipline, people don't try

Many managers fail because they do not have the self-discipline to succeed. As a manager, for some of the time you need to do what you should do, rather than what you want to do. And you must remain this self-disciplined, setting a consistent example. Why is this so important? Because your team is watching you. They conclude that what you do is what you deem to be acceptable behaviour.

Many managers expect their team to *do what I say, not what I do*. For example, some managers arrive late but expect their team to arrive on time. The team will pay lip service to requests to arrive on time, but silently reason, *'What is OK for the boss must be OK for me.'*

You set the standards that your team aspires to, whether you intend it or not. Your team will aspire to be almost as good as you are, so if your standards are low, their standards will be slightly lower! And then you have a problem.

If your personal standards slip in one area, it is reasonable for your team to expect that you will also tolerate slippage in other areas. Let's say that you promise your team that you will do so-and-so by next week and you don't. Obviously, you cannot complain when other people also complete work later than promised. And if you're slack about delivering on promises made, then you are also probably slack about standards and quality.

This does not mean that your team expects you to be perfect, but they do expect you to try. If they see you trying hard, they will forgive you when you occasionally slip. After all, they reason, we're all human.

*'He who knows much may be learned,*
*but he who understands himself is more intelligent.*
*He who controls others may be powerful,*
*but he who has mastered himself is mightier still.'*

*Lao-Tzu*

# Law 28
## All bullies eventually suffer their just rewards

Are you a bully? For the sake of you and your team, let's hope not. Some managers, who admit to being a bully, feel that this honest disclosure excuses their behaviour and makes it acceptable for them to carry on, which it most certainly does not. Many bullies are blind to their own faults and unaware that some of their daily actions constitute bullying. Try this check test.

Look back and be honest with yourself. Have you ever, intentionally or inadvertently, done any of the following to a team member?

- Made persistent negative comments
- Humiliated someone in front of others
- Made verbal threats or verbally intimidated someone
- Made fun of an employee through offensive or abusive personal remarks
- Ostracized or ignored one team member
- Made physical threats or tried to intimidate by appearing physically dominant

All of the above six actions are considered bullying, and rightly so. Employment law in your area may well include a similar list of actions as unlawful, with potentially heavy penalties and the possibility of the authorities awarding punitive damages to the employee.

When you consider your own actions, remember that a more sensitive person will feel the effect of your words or actions in situations where another person who is thicker-skinned and more resilient may not give a damn. For this reason, bullying is principally identified as bullying by the effect on the person at the receiving end, rather than the power of the action taken by the bully.

Managers are placed in positions of authority, which gives them the opportunity (knowingly or unthinkingly) to bully members of their team. Sometimes it appears they can do this with impunity. Companies often turn a blind eye, especially when the manager is currently delivering good results. Bullies may get away with their behaviour for years, while leaving behind them a trail of human distress. It is inevitable, though, that one day all bullies meet someone who suddenly stands up to them.

This person feels that they have endured such personal torment and public humiliation that when they eventually pluck up the courage to fight back they have summoned the resolve to follow through and ensure the bully gets his or her just deserts. Nowadays, employment law comes down very hard on bullies and on the organizations that knowingly or unknowingly allow bullying to take place. The bully can easily find that he or she is out on the street with no job, loss of pension, loss of respect, reduced career prospects and a financially bleak future.

If you have done any of the six things listed above, you must accept the reality that your past actions have included bullying. It may be that your natural style and personality lead you to be a forceful manager. If so, go careful and watch yourself. Sadly, many managers, including some senior managers, confuse unconstructive bullying with being tough and dynamic. They are misguided and reduce their achievements, because nobody consistently gives of their best when they feel bullied.

*'Authority has always attracted the lowest elements in the human race. All through history mankind has been bullied by scum.'*

*P. J. O'Rourke, b.1947,*
*American political columnist and satirist*

# Law 29

## The team does not judge you by your best or worst performances

Managers make more decisions than other employees, and the outcomes of these decisions are especially visible to scrutiny. Consequently, the highs and lows of your personal performance are on display. This causes many managers to swing from feelings of pure elation to suffering despair and humiliation.

You may just have pulled off the biggest coup of your career so far. Everyone is in awe of your performance. Unfortunately, this adulation will not last for long. And, conversely, things will occasionally go badly for you, so badly that you wonder if perhaps it would be better to move on to another job and start again with a clean slate. But your big blunder will soon fade in people's memories if you bounce back and keep on trying to do your best. You even out the ups and downs into an overall level of performance.

For example, Winston Churchill is universally accepted as having been one of the greatest leaders of all time. Yet his list of failures includes twice deserting his political party (he once described himself as a rat who deserts sinking ships). When in charge of the Royal Navy, Churchill championed the disastrous Dardanelles Campaign of 1915 and he was reviled for the consequential slaughter of Allied troops. And then in 1926, while a government minister, Churchill's actions triggered the biggest labour strike in British history.

These failures were enough to end most careers in obscurity. As he learned lessons in the school of hard knocks, Churchill suffered severe losses of confidence, which he described as his *'black dog days'*. But, because he kept on trying, Churchill's outstanding failures were outweighed by outstanding successes and his overall reputation became that of a great leader and a great success.

People generally want their leaders to succeed. They know it's not easy for you to be the boss and so they accept that occasionally you will make some big mistakes. They can live with that, provided that when things go badly you don't let them down by giving up; and when things go extremely well you don't make the mistake of thinking yourself to be overly important or, even worse, start resting on your laurels. We are the average of our performance over time.

*'Only a mediocre person is always at his best.'*

*W. Somerset Maugham, 1874–1965,*
*British playwright and author*

# Law 30

## The team believe what they see over what you say

A certain very large bank was upgrading their computer system. The migration from the old computer to the new system was generally smooth, but some problems were inevitable. Most seriously, for one week it was impossible for staff at the bank to see all the usual details about customers' accounts, essential information for them to answer customer enquiries satisfactorily.

Customers became frustrated and complained to anyone who would listen. The press got wind of the problem and negative publicity about the bank started to hit staff morale. The bank's senior vice-president (SVP) of operations felt he must do something to raise staff morale – and quickly. This is what he did.

He held an internal telephone conference call with staff. During a professional and persuasive presentation, he claimed the computer migration had been seamless, invisible to the customers, a great success. His performance was so good that by the end of his ten-minute speech many employees felt uplifted and motivated. However, the staff that dealt with customers face to face, or on the telephone, could not reconcile the SVP's positive claims with the fuming customers they encountered every day.

Naturally, they chose to believe the evidence of their own experience.

Within hours of the speech, employees were to be heard commenting, *'You can't trust a thing the bank tells employees'* and, *'They must think we're stupid'* and, *'The bank doesn't care.'* From that day on everything the SVP said was suspected of being untruthful or an attempt to manipulate.

It could be that the SVP was speaking without realizing how serious the customer service problem really was, but staff will not make allowances for such errors. Staff expect managers to find out what is really happening, and rightly so.

If only the presentation had commenced by acknowledging the reality of the difficulties employees faced in satisfying customers, then the outcome could have been so much better.

If your statements are patently untrue in one instance, how can you be relied upon at other times?

Once your team concludes that you are capable of telling those untruths the damage is done, probably permanently. They will not tell you to your face, but forever more they will doubt the sincerity and reliability in all that you say.

The lesson is for you to be very careful that at all times what you say to your team does not conflict with the evidence of their experience.

*'What you are shouts so loudly in my ear, that I cannot hear what you say.'*

*Ralph Waldo Emerson, 1803–1882,*
*American essayist and philosopher*

# Law 31
# Listening to personal stuff can backfire

One of your team approaches you and says, '*I need to speak with you about a personal problem.*' The problem could be '*I feel that I am being sexually harassed by another member of the team*'; or perhaps it could be '*I have a relative who is seriously ill and I can't concentrate on my work*'.

In both the above circumstances, and many more, it is appropriate for the employee to talk to his or her line manager about the problem. You need to handle such approaches very professionally.

If you work for a large organization, there will surely be procedures and guidelines on how you are required to handle any personal problems raised by an employee. All managers are required to comply with employment law, which governs how you deal with these personal work-related issues.

It is a manager's duty to respond to legitimate work-related personal problems such as bullying, harassment, discrimination, work-related stress, etc. It is also a manager's duty to respond with consideration when an employee is temporarily unable to perform as well as usual through personal problems such as illness, bereavement, etc. However, some other situations could lead you into very personal discussions, which will eventually backfire. Here's why.

A narrow boundary exists between learning

enough about an employee to help, and crossing that boundary into personal territory that should only be open to a very close friend or professional counsellor.

Most of us love to talk about ourselves. In the right circumstances, many of us will gushingly reveal our inner feelings and our problems. During a one-to-one meeting, or a relaxed social occasion, you may find that with little encouragement employees will reveal personal information. This makes it all too easy for you to cross the barely visible boundary between professional interest and getting overly personal.

Someone who has shared close personal information with you probably now regards you as a close friend, someone who is on his or her side. Yet, tomorrow you may need to require hard work from this person despite the fact that he or she feels emotionally down. A problem could arise when you face a conflict between what is good for a team member personally and what is good for the team generally. Or you may be directed from above to take action that is unquestionably good for the organization but which negatively affects one team member. A sudden change from close friend to hard and unfeeling boss will make you seem downright schizophrenic!

Be careful not to cross the boundary between professional interest and personal prying. If necessary, control your personal curiosity. Only go down roads where employee discussions stay on a professional level. That way you will be on safe territory: close professional friendship rather than close personal friendship.

> 'To be a leader of men one must turn one's back on men.'
>
> Havelock Ellis, 1859–1939,
> British psychologist

# Law 32

## There is often an unfair time delay between effort and reward

No doubt, you have heard countless stories of how great achievement comes only after determined, persistent effort against all odds: climbing Mount Everest, winning a gold medal at the Olympic Games, etc. We accept that these extraordinary results require an attitude of *'I will never give up!'*

At work, as in all other fields of endeavour, there is often an unfair time lag between effort and results. This is a simple practicality that stems from the naturally over-optimistic view that human beings have about how much effort will be required, how long a job will take and how difficult a task will be. Occasionally, everything goes to plan and we achieve our objective bang on time. These are golden high points in planning our work and working our plan. But on most occasions, life at work just isn't that easy.

People react to this difficulty in two different ways. Some become all the more determined, increase their resolve and try a little harder. These people will go the extra mile to achieve the objective. They do not feel unjustly treated when things don't go as easily as expected, they just dig in and keep going. But they are the minority.

When unexpected obstacles appear, when things go wrong or take longer than anticipated, when extra hard work is required, most of us are susceptible to feeling a little hard done by. The unjust time lag between effort and reward can sap our resolve and tempt us to give up. We must admit the reality that the above describes most people, which is probably why we hold in awe the great achievements of the unstoppable and determined few.

Within your team, you need to recognize the following types of people and manage them accordingly:

### The reluctant starter

This person starts from a negative standpoint. He or she expects every job to be fraught with difficulty and impossible to achieve, so why try to do the impossible, if one can avoid the pain of defeat by never making a start?

### The quick stopper

This person makes a good start, but when obstacles to progress present themselves, he or she becomes too easily discouraged and soon gives up.

### The strong-minded succeeder

This person is great to have around because he or she sees each obstacle as a challenge that the team will overcome or circumvent; it's just a matter of determined effort combined with intelligent thought.

### The dogged persister

This person will usually succeed by keeping straight on as planned, smashing through obstacles with sheer effort and dogged persistence. Nevertheless, he or she will sometimes fail because dogged persistence alone can lead people to keep on trying to do the impossible for much too long, instead of intelligently looking for a way around the current problem.

You get the best from your people resources by employing them wisely. Make sure that the reluctant starter makes a start, the quick stopper becomes re-motivated and redirected, the dogged persister is helped to see the way around obstacles and the strong-minded succeeder is given a key influential role in the most challenging jobs.

Teach all of your team the simple fact of life that there is often a seemingly unfair time lag between effort and reward. Your team is not going to allow this to influence you all to give up when later, with hindsight, you will see that you were probably just short of the winning line. Your team does not quit when trying to achieve the achievable. Together, you find the ways around, over or through all obstacles to progress.

'Every obstacle yields to stern resolve. He who is fixed to a star does not change his mind.'

Leonardo da Vinci, 1452–1519,
Italian polymath: scientist, mathematician, engineer,
inventor, anatomist, painter, sculptor, architect, botanist,
musician and writer

# Law 33
# Most people resist planning

Most people resist making plans or implementing them. This statement sounds ridiculous, because we all know that if we create a well-thought-out plan and then we implement it, we are much more likely to succeed. So why should anyone, let alone the majority of people, object to planning? The reason is simple.

No matter how carefully conceived, plans always fail to some degree. In almost every case, something goes wrong. In the worst cases, the objective is never achieved. Most plans contain flaws and even the best-laid plans inevitably fail to account for some unforeseeable glitch. Perhaps during the execution of the plan, circumstances beyond your control require you to adapt and re-plan to get back on track.

Dwight D. Eisenhower described this essential conflict between the certainty that plans will fail and his conviction that planning is essential. He said: *'Plans are worthless, but planning is indispensable.'*

Thus, even the most successful plans carry with them some experience of failure. Naturally, people resist failure; consequently many people resist having anything to do with plans or planning.

Does this phenomenon affect your team? Here's a checklist:

- Do all your current major objectives have well-laid plans to help you achieve them?
- Are you and your team putting all of your plans into operation?
- Are you monitoring progress against the plans?
- Are you adapting your plans to cope with unexpected obstacles along the way?

If the answer to one or more of these questions is 'No' then you are probably resisting planning.

Typical excuses include: '*We don't have time for planning*', '*Our work is so specialist that planning is inappropriate*' or '*We need to react to events all the time, so planning is not possible.*' These typical nonsense statements highlight avoidance strategies.

Except for the minor tasks that arise today and are dealt with immediately, planning your work and working your plan is the essential first step on the road to accomplishing any major objective. One commonly accepted ratio for time saved against time invested in planning is 15:1, so the busier you are the more you need to make time for planning. The old proverb says, '*Failing to plan is planning to fail.*' Trite, but true.

*'He who every morning plans the transaction of the day and follows out that plan carries a thread that will guide him through the maze of the most busy life. But where no plan is laid, where the disposal of time is surrendered merely to the chance of incidence, chaos will soon reign.'*

*Victor Hugo, 1802–1885,*
*French poet, playwright, novelist, essayist,*
*statesman and human rights activist*

# Law 34

# Teams rarely achieve things
# when they believe they can't

To reach the top in athletics an athlete engages in mental as well as physical training. The athlete needs to truly believe that he or she can jump a few inches higher or run a little faster. The belief is an essential part of attaining the goal. After winning gold, you hear them say, '*I knew I could do it.*'

Similarly, in all aspects of life we rarely achieve feats that surprise us. Maybe a few times in a lifetime we put in a sparkling performance and think to ourselves, '*Wow, where did that come from?*' But these occasions are rare. When we think, '*I don't think I can do that,*' we are usually correct.

Our disbelief causes our mental and physical effort to be subtly reduced. Under the surface, our lack of confidence knocks the edge off our performance, and even despite hard work, we are not surprised when the results turn out to be disappointing.

The same is true for teams. In fact, it takes only one disbeliever in a team to sap the confidence and thus prevent the team from achieving their goals and objectives. This team dynamic raises an important question: if only one dissenter can scotch success, then how can your team ever hope to achieve ambitious and stretching objectives?

Following these steps will help resolve the problem:

- Objectives need to be realistic. It is very hard to get people to believe they can achieve the impossible, so double-check that your goals, though stretching, are realistic
- Satisfy yourself beyond doubt that you believe the team's goals are achievable, building your personal belief, then . . .
- Sell your belief: explain, enthuse and convince. Do whatever you must to ensure everyone involved is on-board and therefore capable of success
- Ensure that belief does not slip, by regularly affirming the attainment of each goal. Do this according to the culture of your team. If dancing, joy and shouting are the style of your team, go for it. If a more subdued approach suits better, then frequently and quietly re-enforce the belief with your assured and positive conversation
- Be sensitive to disbelief. There may be members of your team who hold back on giving their true opinion. Instead, you find clues to their lack of belief from small things, such as comments like *'I'll try'* or *'We'll do our best'*. You may notice the body language of folded arms and shrunken posture when discussing the goal. These clues are not in themselves proof, merely indications of inner feelings. Be aware of them. If you discover pockets of disbelief, tackle the problem. Do not consider any lack of faith as the fault of the employee. Get to the root of the reason for their

disbelief. You should be able to correct their misunderstanding. If, instead, they convince you that the goal is genuinely unrealistic, you have learned something of value

• When attempting one big stretching goal that appears to be beyond reach, split the goal into smaller steps, each of which is easier to believe as achievable

Most important of all, always exude confidence and enthusiasm. It's infectious.

---

*'Whether you think that you can, or that you can't, you are usually right.'*

*Attributed to Henry Ford, 1863–1947,*
*founder of the Ford Motor Company*

# Law 35

## Team goals + team desire = team results

'*Success is goals, all else is mere commentary,*' said Henry Ford, and he knew what he was talking about. Ford's seemingly limitless ambitions drove him to set and achieve personal goals that profoundly changed the world in which we live today.

At a time when railway lines were spreading across the world to offer an alternative to travelling by horse, donkey or camel, Ford announced this goal: '*I will belt the Earth with affordable, reliable automobiles.*' For the first time in industry, Ford created mass production methods which he introduced into his factory. The effect of his methods slashed the cost of production. In 1909, you would have paid $825 to buy the Model T Runabout. By 1927, the price was down to only $360. As a result, almost a hundred years later, the rusting remains of the ubiquitous Model T Ford can be found everywhere in the world; and many of these motorcars are still driven by enthusiast owners. Henry Ford's personal goals single-handedly set the stage for the world's current love affair with the motorcar.

Ford was not the only goal-oriented person in his company. He inspired complete teams of people, notably engineers, to become passionately committed to achieving team objectives. For example, the Ford V-8 engine block (introduced in March 1932) was cast as one piece of iron. The technology to achieve this one-piece casting did not hitherto exist. The Ford team of engineers sweated for two years until they discovered the key to casting this complex piece of metal. Afterwards, Henry Ford declared their breakthrough to be the inevitable outcome, once the entire team passionately wanted to achieve the goal.

Compare the above example to your own experience. Think back to the occasions in your life when you passionately desired to achieve something. The more we contemplate the joy of achieving our goal the more determined we become. The goal moves from being a merely rational objective to an emotional feeling. Fervent desire builds as we picture the achievement of our goal. This fervent desire overrides other considerations and switches on aspects of our character that help us to achieve our goal. For instance, we become more conscious of not wasting time (so our time management improves); and we devote time to thinking about easy ways to get there quickly (we become more creative). These things are true for every individual, and they remain true for a collection of individuals, a team.

Conversely, consider how you feel about spending good time and effort in trying to achieve something that you believe will honestly never happen – not very enthusiastic, I expect. These negative feelings knock the edge off performance. In fact, although fellow team members may go through the motions of working on achieving goals that they do not believe in, the quality and quantity of their effort is much reduced.

This does not mean that if you whip up a fantasy enthusiasm about the improbable and unachievable it will magically come into being. No, balanced professional judgement is your starting point. But as soon as you are convinced an objective is achievable, you need to build a collective team desire to attain the goal. In our rational and analytical business world, this fundamental emotional aspect of team performance is too often overlooked.

You will achieve much more from your team if you devote time, energy and thought to making sure that:

- You wholeheartedly believe in the goal. You feel emotionally enthused, committed and convinced that it can be achieved
- Every team member believes it can be done
- Most of all, you need every team member to genuinely desire to achieve the goal. You foster this desire by building a positive picture of how it will feel when the goal is achieved

Meet these three conditions and you unleash team performance at a higher level of determination, creativeness and productivity than most managers get out of their teams in an entire lifetime.

'If one advances confidently in the direction of their dreams, and endeavors to lead a life which they have imagined, they will meet with a success unexpected in common hours.'

*Henry David Thoreau, 1817–1862,*
*American author, poet, naturalist, development critic,*
*surveyor, historian and philosopher*

# Law 36
## Few people think, really think

Even when our conscious mind is subdued by sleep, it continues working away behind the scenes. So, biologically speaking, we never stop thinking. However, this does not mean that our thoughts are focused, controlled, well directed and creative, which is the quality of thought we need for solving problems at work, or making the best decisions, or creating new ideas.

Except for a few gifted people, most of us need to make a considerable effort to enable our brain to switch into any one of its most effective modes of thought. This can be hard work, especially if our brain is not accustomed to us expecting it to perform on demand. As Henry Ford said, *'Thinking is the hardest work there is, which is the probable reason why so few engage in it.'*

Look around at examples of excellent levels of performance. In sport, for example, people at the top of their game possess excellent physique, timing, power and speed, plus the ability to outwit their competition. Listen attentively to interviews of people at the highest levels of attainment in any sphere and you will hear the output from a finely tuned brain, seeing through the fog of life (analytical ability) to find new solutions to problems (creativity).

Here is a team exercise that uses several thinking styles for analysis and creativity. It should help you make a significant step forward with your team.

For this mental workout, your team needs to be somewhere away from all interruptions. Give each of the four steps at least twenty minutes of your undivided and concentrated attention. You can split the exercise into several sessions, but do not allow your mind to become distracted while you focus upon each question. Force the mind to discard all extraneous thoughts. If you notice your attention wandering off the subject, drag it back to the matter in hand. It is important that you complete the exercise exactly as instructed.

## Step 1. Brainstorm One

Look back over recent events at work and the performance of you and your team. Pose the question: *What do you feel prevents us all from achieving as much as we would wish to accomplish each day?*

Make a list, not a short list. Don't be satisfied with the obvious few things that immediately spring to mind. Make sure your list includes everything it should, possibly even the one item that is potentially very significant, but has never before crossed your mind.

As a guide, if your list contains fewer than twenty items you're not trying hard enough. Keep digging for significant items you may have missed; either because they are accepted as the unchangeable norm, or because they are such an ingrained habit that they are never pondered over.

## Step 2. Analyse

Of the blocks to performance you have listed, consider which, when removed, would have the most positive effect on results. Draw up a shortlist. Next, prioritize your shortlist so that you can confidently answer this question: *What is the single most important block to performance which, if removed, would create the maximum possible surge in achievement and results?*

## Step 3. Brainstorm Two

Your next task is to come up with possible solutions. *What is the single most important block to performance that you identified in step 2?* The solutions you list should be actions that are within your power and authority to put into practice.

To make your brainstorming sessions more fruitful, you must not allow people to criticize any suggestion, no matter how silly it might appear to be. Criticism kills creativity stone dead (even if it is purely you alone internally criticizing your own ideas). Your level of creativity is raised when you are working hard, but also when you are enjoying yourself. So, if crazy, amusing ideas come to mind just add them to the list. Accelerate your pace. Think of, and list, the ideas as fast as you can scribble them down. The quality of ideas does not matter just now; quantity is more important.

Eventually, people's minds will start to slow down and offer up fewer ideas, but at this stage do not stop until you have squeezed those little grey cells absolutely dry.

Next, separate the creative phase from the forthcoming analytical phase with another short break. Have a pen and paper with you during this break because, if you have been concentrating sufficiently hard, your brain will surely, at some unexpected moment while you are relaxed and least expect it, drop into your conscious attention an absolute pearl of a thought. Write down this thought immediately. Don't risk losing it, because later you will probably fail to recall this little gem. Strangely, these afterthoughts usually prove to be very original and constructive.

Step 4. Analyse and Decide

By now, you should have a list of the things that prevent you from achieving as much as you would wish to accomplish each day. You should have identified the single most important block to performance, which if removed would create the maximum possible surge in achievement and results. And you should have a list of possible solutions to remove the single most important block to performance that you identified.

Your task now is to analyse critically your list of solutions. Discard the truly unworkable and unrealistic. Delete any remaining ideas that fall outside your power and ability to implement. The remaining shortlist of items will all be good ideas. Finally, prioritize this shortlist according to their effectiveness.

A few of these ideas will be practical and you can immediately make use of them. You should find at least one idea that, provided you execute it, will significantly improve the daily output of you and your team. You may even have created an entirely new idea that will be a real winner for you.

When people go through the above exercise for the first time, some find it difficult to concentrate their attention fully on the matter at hand. They find they do not have the ability to call their brain to order, and their brain is lazy in responding with creativity. This does not mean they cannot be creative, but it does mean that this ability is currently lying dormant through lack of use.

Research shows that our brains give out the most creative ideas when they act in a single pointed mode of concentration. However, if your brain is not accustomed to thinking in this disciplined way, it fights off your attempt to switch into focused concentration mode, though everybody is capable of creating practical ideas of excellent vision and value.

Nearly all of us will improve our management performance by honing our thinking skills, especially if we tap into the potential of the rarely used resources that exist in the combined thinking capacity of a team.

'If one wants to be successful, one must think; one must think until it hurts. One must worry a problem in one's mind until it seems there cannot be another aspect of it that hasn't been considered.'

Roy Herbert Thomson, 1894–1976,
Canadian newspaper proprietor
and media entrepreneur

# Law 37
## Energy levels rise and fall with expectations

There are times when we are brimful of vibrant energy. Look back; the periods of your highest energy coincide with the times when you were confident of your progress towards a positive conclusion.

The same is true for groups of people, but with an added bonus. When surrounded by people who also feel energized, we feed off each other. Energy levels climb even higher, the work seems easier, our stamina increases and we brush aside the inevitable minor setbacks and tribulations that we meet along the way.

When the leader confidently expects a positive result, the team senses this self-assurance. It is visible in the leader's body language and the little comments that exude confidence and energy. And it's catching. It's no good trying to fake this confidence. That's acting, and you cannot convincingly keep up the act full-time. So, how do you make sure that you genuinely feel confident and enthusiastic? The answer is to make sure that you really do believe you are going to achieve the team goals.

If you think the targets are unrealistic, check them out for yourself. Has it been done before; who did it; how; when? Does your team contain the required expertise and resources? If not, can you acquire the necessary skills and knowledge? This questioning and planning phase is an essential step towards building a high level of personal enthusiasm and confidence, so don't skimp on the job.

When you have successfully passed through this period of questioning and planning you can rise to the challenge ahead with increased confidence. That confidence increases your expectation of success, which pumps up your energy levels. Now you can talk openly of your confidence and let all the members of your team share the feeling. Energy levels will start rising and productivity levels will soon follow.

'If you expect the best, you will be the best. Learn to use one of the most powerful laws in this world; change your mental habits to belief instead of disbelief.'

Norman Vincent Peale, 1898–1993,
American Protestant preacher and author

# Law 38

## People don't get out of bed
## to achieve *your* goals

Studies of human personality have shown that across the world about a quarter of us feel driven towards setting and achieving personal goals. The remaining three-quarters are not naturally goal-driven people and they get their personal fulfilment from other motivational factors.

If you are a goal-directed person you naturally carry the desire to set and achieve goals in all areas of your life, and this strongly influences how you approach your work.

The easiest way to identify who in your team is naturally goal-directed is for you and your team to complete personal psychometric test questionnaires. The results of these tests provide valuable insights into a person's behaviour at work. Recruiters have been using these tests for decades as a guide to matching jobs and people.

If a psychometric questionnaire is not an option for you, then you need to use your own judgement to identify who in your team is driven to achieve personal goals. Visible traits of a goal-directed person might include them appearing conscientious, self-motivated, focused, assertive, enthusiastic and independent.

Goal-directed people are a great asset to your team because they are self-starters who will try hard to achieve the objectives. However, one caution: be aware that if there were a conflict between company goals and personal goals, the personal goals would take priority.

The majority of people are not so driven. At home, their motivation may centre on family life or personal hobbies and passions. This means that some of your team come to work primarily out of the necessity to earn money. Your desperate desire for team members to work extra hard to achieve the goals that you set could be of little real interest to them.

This does not mean that your people are incapable of hard work, or being enthusiastic, or doing a good job – far from it. But it does mean that when you expect everybody in your team to become passionate about achieving the team goals you may be in for a disappointment. Some people will make the right noises and look keen, just for your benefit, while below the surface they remain uninspired. So, how do you motivate them to go the extra mile, to make the extra effort that you need from them?

One key lies in the pleasure that everyone enjoys from completing a job well done, something to feel proud of. Therefore, you praise and encourage quality work.

A second motivator is to exchange effort for praise. Therefore, when team members work hard, you praise good effort, even on occasions when the effort achieves relatively little.

Another key to motivation lies in the fact that we

humans are gregarious creatures. We enjoy company and we especially enjoy achieving things together. When we work together to achieve things, we cannot help but have feelings of inner satisfaction. Achieving things together is the glue that instantly bonds relationships; it is the essence that creates team spirit. Therefore, you praise what you all achieve together, not as a result of you telling them what to do but through them working together with your guidance and support.

For example, in sales it may prove impossible to fire up a team to achieve the company's financial targets, yet that same team will work like crazy in order to feel part of a team that others admire and respect for giving good service. And, of course, sales rise because of that service. The satisfaction of doing their job well vastly exceeds the feelings enjoyed by adding zeros to the tail of a number.

The above is true in all occupations. So, if your team appears to be less than excited about striving to achieve the goals that you set, take heart. And take stock of the tasks carried out by your team. Select the activities that, when done well, will bring feelings of satisfaction every day. Identify the smaller tasks that will lead to achieving the big, long-term goals and, through careful use of justly deserved praise, engender a culture where team members go home at the end of the day feeling personally proud of the effort they have put in, of a job well done and of belonging to the team.

'When dealing with people, let us remember we are not dealing with creatures of logic. We are dealing with creatures of emotion, creatures bustling with prejudices and motivated by pride and vanity.'

Dale Carnegie, 1888–1955,
American developer of world-renowned
self-improvement courses

# Law 39

## There are nine common de-motivators

It's all too easy to de-motivate people, crushing their enthusiasm and negating all other efforts to motivate and manage them. The cause is usually a lack of forethought by the manager, or not appreciating the strong negative effect caused by the following common de-motivators.

### 1. Persistent criticism

When things go wrong and the manager feels cross, it is very easy to lash out at the person who immediately appears to be at fault. If the manager regularly criticizes one person, it de-motivates not only the person receiving the criticism but also other team members who witness it. Make it a policy never to criticize in anger or haste, but first to understand the true situation and the true culprit. If you repeatedly need to reprimand the same person, you must find an alternative solution.

### 2. Unattainable targets

When the manager has a habit of setting unattainable targets, it kills all motivation stone dead. People quickly learn that no matter how hard they try, they are doomed to failure. Plan carefully, understand all the implications and convince yourself that all the targets are achievable.

Setting unattainable goals is one of the dirtier

tricks used by unscrupulous managers to bully an employee or pressurize them into leaving. The team easily spots this tactic. They wonder, *'Will I be next?'* which creates a broad and long-lasting negative effect on overall performance.

### 3. Changing targets, thus making it impossible to succeed

Consider this scenario. Recently announced targets were a challenge at the time of their introduction, but circumstances have changed. Unforeseen events have made the targets easy to achieve, almost a certainty. They are no longer a spur to activity and fail to exploit potential new opportunities. The solution is unavoidable: targets will have to rise mid-term.

The problem comes when some people have already enjoyed the emotional high of savouring their personal forthcoming success. They may have (unwisely) already spent their future bonuses, sharing the excitement with loved ones. If they learn that this joy is to be taken away and replaced by raised targets and hard work, some people will feel cheated.

One effective way to minimize this negative effect is to cut short the existing target period. Praise achievements to date, celebrate the success and hand out fair and proportional rewards for achievements made so far. Then, pause for a day or so to provide adequate time to enjoy the success. Afterwards, announce the new target period, the new targets and any new bonus or rewards scheme.

## 4. Withholding material information, thus making it near impossible to succeed

Managers frequently fail to pass on all the essential information, through poor delegation technique, inadequate support during a project or failure to think things through in detail. The worst offenders tend to be those managers who adopt a general policy of sharing information on a strictly need-to-know basis.

- When you delegate important objectives and tasks, confirm the delegation in writing. One side of letter paper is the maximum. More text won't get read or remembered. Delegating in writing is a discipline that forces you to consider carefully all the detail involved and the knowledge and information required to achieve the objective

- Don't rush delegation. Allow time for the person to ask questions, immediately or later. This is one of the many areas where it pays to allocate adequate time to ensure that you do it right first time

- Don't delegate and forget. Schedule an appropriate degree of supervision so that you have the opportunity to provide extra support or missing information as the work progresses

## 5. The manager picks on one person where there is a wider problem

Being the only one criticized when the fault also

lies with others is an injustice that many people feel intensely. Here are two common causes with suggested solutions:

1.  *Personal dislike*
    When we don't warm to a person, it is all too easy to direct our venom disproportionately at that one person. We know that we should be even-handed, but sometimes we act instinctively. If you find that you are not particularly fond of one team member, adjust your opinion by listing that person's positive attributes and values to your team.

2.  *Instant reprimands*
    If a manager reacts immediately to a problem, lashing out with an instant rebuke, there is a fair chance the manager will get it wrong. The individual who received the telling-off may not personally have made the mistake. Sometimes he or she happened to be working at the point where the mistake became visible. Before issuing a reprimand, pause and check, '*Is this person the root cause, or merely the visible effect of a wider problem or a hidden problem?*'

## 6. Intrusive monitoring of work

If you apply too little supervision, people are apt to do the wrong things, the wrong way, at the wrong time. Conversely, when you direct every move, check every detail and suppress a person's discretion to act alone, then you remove all feelings of fulfilment for that person. And you make yourself so busy that you may as well do the work yourself.

Finding the correct balance is not easy, but you are more likely to get it right when you aim for all decisions to be taken at the lowest practical level in your organization. Train your team so that in your absence they will always act as you would wish them to.

## 7. Undervalue work done

If you ignore a person's contribution, making no comment or giving no praise, very soon they start wondering why they try so hard. Why not do the minimum, because their contribution goes unnoticed anyway? Could any of your team feel like that?

If you tend to give little feedback, it's easy to address this personal trait by making a daily habit of catching people doing a good job, which gives you the opportunity to say '*Well done*'. In addition, review the achievements of the past week. Who has done a good job, maintained standards, improved quality or achieved something special? Praise in public whenever possible because it only takes a moment, costs nothing and is one of the most powerful motivators.

## 8. The manager claims the credit for someone else's work

Occasionally, a manager grabs all the credit in the hope of currying favour and gaining promotion. This is probably an unwise tactic, because in stealing a person's accomplishments, the manager de-motivates the team and reduces future achievements. And when senior management reviews performance, they are more likely to promote a manager who has created a team of talented people.

Some managers claim credit for good ideas because they believe the ideas were their own, when actually some of the team thought them up. This easily happens when a new idea receives much discussion and deliberation before implementation. By the time the manager decides to implement the new idea, he or she cannot remember where the idea came from and thinks it was his or her own, which is a severe de-motivator.

Confident and strong managers work on the principle that they take the blame when things go wrong, but their team gets the credit when things go right. The result of this policy is that team members feel they are part of a united family with a confident and caring leader. And that is a sound foundation upon which to build a very productive team.

## 9. Removing an area of responsibility without justification

Reorganizing who handles each responsibility is

occasionally inevitable. People generally accept that. However, status matters, so that if you remove from someone a valued responsibility and do not replace it with an equal or greater responsibility, that person will resent the change and become de-motivated.

If there is no just cause – such as the responsibility being no longer required, or the person was failing to discharge the responsibility satisfactorily – the person will probably also feel that you have treated them unjustly and harbour resentment.

If you promote a person into a new responsibility and then fail to support them or enable them to succeed, and then subsequently remove the responsibility, that person will feel they have been unfairly set up to fail.

A manager has a professional duty to do his or her best to ensure that people are capable of handling the extra responsibilities that they have been given. If not, it would be wise to coach, mentor and support the employee until they are equal to the task.

---

*'Reorganization is a wondrous thing, creating the illusion of decisive action and instant progress, while actually changing very little, except to spread fear, uncertainty and doubt.'*

*Caius Porteus, Roman senator,*
*during a speech to the Senate, AD 22*

# Law 40

# Many managers do not truly
# want to be the boss

The final law of management is concerned with neither management nor leadership but with your personality. Is your true personality, your deeply ingrained concept of yourself, truly suited to controlling and managing others? Does being the leader come naturally to you, so that others feel inspired to follow, or are you finding that the responsibility weighs very heavy right now?

Many of us really do not want the responsibility of being the boss. At heart, we prefer others to lead the way and take the blame when things go wrong. And why not? Taking full responsibility for our own actions is often sufficient challenge without accepting additional responsibility for the actions of other people.

Often, we accept the responsibility because we need the extra money. Maybe we feel our career progress has halted and management seems the next logical step. It could be that we are the longest-serving and most knowledgeable person in the department, so we slide into the manager's position by default. And when offered the job most people feel it would be foolish to turn down such an opportunity. Many aspire to the title, the kudos, the extra pay, but not the responsibility. And this creates an inner conflict.

To handle this inner conflict some managers fool themselves into believing they take full responsibility when actually they avoid it. Their team soon perceive this deficiency, and this impinges on performance because although people will give their best for a true leader they will only do half their best for half a leader. And teams that run at half-throttle are heading towards failure.

If you feel unsure as to whether you are cut out to be a leader, don't immediately give up. A small number of people are naturals at balancing the different skills of managing and controlling with those of inspiring and leading. But the vast majority of us can dramatically improve our results, and make life as a manager much easier, simply through working towards the high standards described in this book.

It is only after working at improving our management skills, knowledge and attitude that many of us discover a latent ability for leading others. If, after considerable effort, you still feel unsure, then examine your own intent, listening carefully to the small, quiet voice from within. Do you truly desire to be an effective manager and an excellent leader?

If the answer is no, then you may well find that in order to be a successful manager you have to step too far outside your natural personality and that over time you pay a heavy price. Perhaps management is not for you. There are many other ways to earn a good living and many other paths to personal fulfilment.

If the answer is yes, you truly do desire to become

an excellent leader, when you act in accordance with the secret laws of management it's actually not that difficult. It helps if you have an insatiable desire for the role. It helps if you naturally possess the qualities and the habits required.

However, look around at the standard of the management you see at work. Generally, it is rather disappointing. This means that if you work diligently at becoming a better manager and leader, you can easily stand far above the crowd. Management and leadership is not rocket science; it's mostly common sense.

With committed effort and by facing up to the unavoidable realities of management described in this book, any manager can lift his or her performance to new heights, make their job much easier and in the process feel much happier at work.

'Press on: nothing in the world can take the place of persistence – talent will not – genius will not – education will not. Persistence and determination alone are omnipotent.'

Calvin Coolidge, 1872–1933,
30th President of the United States of America

## From problem to solution

| Management problem | Likely causes and solutions |
|---|---|
| *One member of my team is demanding too much of my time . . .* | Law 14 |
| *I don't know how best to handle a team member who has approached me about his or her personal problems . . .* | Law 31 |
| *My team needs to be more enthusiastic . . .* | Laws: 1, 16, 26, 30, 34, 35, 37, 38, 39 |
| *My team is resisting changes that I know we must make . . .* | Laws: 10, 30, 33, 39 |
| *Someone in my team makes silly mistakes. They just seem to act stupidly on occasions . . .* | Laws: 12, 21, 28, 39 |
| *Some, or all, of us continually feel tired and worn out . . .* | Laws: 13, 18, 24, 38, 39 |

| | |
|---|---|
| *My team has made some mistakes and hidden them from me. By the time I learn about the problems, the situation has become serious . . .* | Laws: 15, 28, 39 |
| *Recently, I feel that I have failed to live up to the standards I expect of myself as a manager . . .* | Laws: 2, 26, 27, 28, 29, 39, 40 |
| *Some of my team just won't make decisions for themselves, even when I tell them to . . .* | Laws: 2, 26, 27, 28, 39 |
| *My team is not achieving enough . . .* | Laws: 2, 3, 4, 5, 6, 8, 9, 17, 18, 19, 20, 24, 27, 28, 32, 33, 34, 35, 37, 39 |
| *There is no time for planning because every day we are too busy coping with the work . . .* | Laws: 2, 3, 6, 13, 18, 19, 24, 25, 33, 35 |
| *Some of my team repeatedly fail to deliver on their promises . . .* | Laws: 2, 3, 6, 8, 18, 23, 27, 32, 33, 34, 39 |

| | |
|---|---|
| *The work takes much longer than expected . . .* | Laws: 2, 3, 5, 6, 8, 12, 17, 18, 19, 24, 32, 33, 34, 35, 37 |
| *Initially my team is excited about each new objective, but soon the enthusiasm fades away . . .* | Laws: 2, 34, 35, 37, 39 |
| *My boss expects my team to achieve things much faster than I believe is possible . . .* | Laws: 2, 5, 6, 8, 24, 33 |
| *Occasionally, team members show signs of being cross with me . . .* | Laws: 2, 5, 7, 10, 11, 12, 16, 19, 20, 26, 27, 28, 30, 31, 39 |
| *Some of our major projects seem impossible to achieve . . .* | Laws: 2, 5, 8, 18, 19, 24, 33, 34, 35, 37 |
| *Some of my team frequently arrive late for work . . .* | Laws: 26, 27, 38, 39 |
| *Some of my team have a bad attitude . . .* | Laws: 26, 39 |
| *I'm beginning to wonder if I am really cut out to be a manager . . .* | Laws: 29, 40 |

| | |
|---|---|
| *It looks like we're going to fail to achieve an important objective on time . . .* | Laws: 3, 5, 6, 8, 18, 23, 24, 27, 33, 34, 37, 38, 39 |
| *We are not getting on with our most important tasks because of all the interruptions . . .* | Laws: 3, 6, 13, 18, 19, 33 |
| *There are just not enough hours in the day . . .* | Laws: 3, 8, 18, 19, 24, 25, 33, 34, 35 |
| *Some of my team tend to avoid or delay getting started on their tasks . . .* | Laws: 3, 9, 35, 37, 38, 39 |
| *I suspect that my team does not believe what I am saying . . .* | Laws: 30, 31, 39 |
| *My team appears to be uninterested in objectives . . .* | Laws: 4, 5, 26, 27, 28, 34, 37, 38, 39 |
| *My team is making too many mistakes . . .* | Laws: 5, 12, 13, 26, 27, 39 |
| *We are not as organized as I believe we should be . . .* | Laws: 5, 13, 18, 19, 24, 33, 34, 35, 36 |

*I delegate a task, I expect progress, but they just don't get on with the work . . .*     Laws: 5, 6, 16, 18, 34, 26, 27, 33, 34, 35, 37, 38, 39

*One of my very best people has suddenly started making mistakes or falling behind in his or her work . . .*     Laws: 5, 6, 8, 12, 20, 39

*Sometimes, one of my team is working on a task for another manager, while the work I gave him or her remains untouched . . .*     Laws: 6, 13, 16, 18, 19

*My team doesn't seem to trust me . . .*     Laws: 7, 8, 10, 27, 28, 30, 39

*Our plans are inadequate or inaccurate . . .*     Laws: 8, 18, 19, 24, 32, 33, 34, 36

*I have problems with someone being lazy . . .*     Laws: 9, 11, 15, 21, 22, 23, 27, 32, 34, 37, 38, 39

*My team spends too much time socializing and not enough time doing the work . . .*     Laws: 9, 14, 26, 27, 35, 37, 38, 39

# Index